Siraj
May 1, 2011
Atlanta

D1572890

آ ئیے اردو پڑھیں

Let's Study Urdu

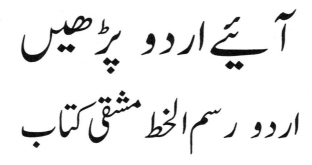

Let's Study Urdu

An Introduction to the Script

Ali S. Asani

Harvard University

and

Syed Akbar Hyder

University of Texas, Austin

Yale University Press

New Haven and London

Copyright © 2008 by Yale University

All rights reserved

This book may not be reproduced, in whole or part, including illustrations, in any form (beyond that copying permitted by Sections 107 and 108 of the U.S. Copyright Law and except by reviewers for the public press), without written permission from the publishers.

Publisher: Mary Jane Peluso

Development Editor: Brie Kluytenaar

Manuscript Editor: Noreen O'Connor-Abel

Production Editor: Ann-Marie Imbornoni

Production Controller: Karen Stickler

Marketing Manager: Timothy Shea

Cover Design: Mary Valencia

Cover Photograph: Michael Currier

Printed in the United States of America.

ISBN 978-0-300-12060-8 (pbk.: alk.paper)

Library of Congress Control Number: 2006939859

A catalogue record for this book is available from the British Library.

The paper in this book meets the guidelines for permanence and durability of the Committee on Production Guidelines for Book Longevity of the Council on Library Resources.

10 9 8 7 6 5 4 3 2

Contents

Introduction   viii

The Letters of the Urdu Alphabet   1

Unit One

The Urdu Script   3

1.1 The letter "*alif*" ا and the short vowels   3

1.2 The "*be*" series   4

1.3 Unfriendly and friendly letters   5

1.4 The letters of the "*be*" series with "*alif*"   8

1.5 Two more letters -- "*nuun*" and "*choTii ye*"   8

1.6 "*Alif madda*"   9

Unit Two

2.1 The "*jiim*" series   11

2.2 Letters of the "*jiim*" series with "*alif*"   13

2.3 "*ChoTii ye*" as "*ii*" vowel   14

2.4 The letter "*wao*" or "*vav*" as a consonant   15

2.5 The letter "*wao*" as a vowel   16

Unit Three

3.1 "*Barii ye*" as a vowel   19

3.2 Medial forms of "*choTii ye*" and "*baRii ye*"   20

3.3 The letters "*kaaf*," "*gaaf*," and "*laam*"   22

3.4 Independent forms of vowels   24

Unit Four

4.1 The "*daal*" series   27

4.2 The "*re*" series   29

4.3 The letter "*miim*"   31

4.4 The "*hamza*" at vowel junctions   33

Unit Five

5.1 The letters "*fe*" and "*qaaf*"   36

5.2 "*ChoTii he*"   38

5.3 "*ChoTii he*" and pronunciation   40

5.4 "*Do cashmii he*" and aspiration   41

Unit Six

6.1 The "*siin*" series   45

6.2 The "*swaad*" and "*to'e*" series   48

6.3 "*Nuun ghunna*" and nasalization   50

Unit Seven

7.1 The letters "*ain*" and "*ghain*"   53

7.2 Note on pronunciation of "*ain*"   54

7.3 Orthographic signs: the "*jazm*" or "*sukuun*"   55

7.4 Orthographic signs: the "*tashdiid*"   57

7.5 Orthographic signs: the "*tanwiin*"   58

7.6 Other orthographic signs   59

7.7 Urdu numerals   59

Urdu Script Workbook   62

Introduction

This book is intended as a primer on reading and writing the Urdu script. For those with little or no knowledge of Urdu, the book may be used in conjunction with its companion volume, *Let's Study Urdu: An Introductory Course,* as an integral part of a beginning course on the Urdu language. It may also be used independently by those who already know how to speak Urdu and who wish to read and write it.

The book does not present the Urdu writing system in strict alphabetical order. Rather, it introduces letters grouped according to commonalities in shape. In this regard, it has adapted the approach used by John Gumperz and C.M. Naim in their *Urdu Reader* (Berkeley: Center for South Asian Studies, University of California, 1960). The introduction to the script has been designed to facilitate a gradual but cumulative learning of the script with as little reliance on transliteration into the Latin alphabet as possible. The letters are introduced in seven units, each of which is divided into several sections. Each section introduces students to a particular letter or element of the writing system. After some illustrative examples, students are presented with reading and writing drills that have been constructed to ensure ease of recognition of newly introduced characters and features. The exercises, in particular those in the earlier units, often contain made-up "nonsense" words in order to expose students to as wide a variety of letter combinations and positions as possible. As the students become more familiar with the script, however, the exercises of later units contain a great portion of actual Urdu vocabulary. Some exercises include common English words and names that are challenging and interesting to read when written in the Urdu script. To assist in pronunciation, a CD containing recordings of the reading exercises of all units accompanies the book. Following Unit Seven, there is a script workbook with a series of calligraphed writing exercises that direct students how to write these letters in aesthetically pleasing ways. We would like to acknowledge the contributions of Junaid Ashraf who calligraphed these writing exercises. Finally, we are deeply grateful to several generations of our students who have been so patient as we experimented with better and more effective ways to teach the script. The comments and invaluable suggestions of various colleagues and fellow teachers of Urdu are also most sincerely appreciated. We would like to acknowledge, in particular, Shahnaz Hassan of University of Texas, Austin, Amy Bard of University of Florida, Naseem Hines of Harvard, Shafique Virani of University of Toronto, Neelima Shukla-Bhatt of Wellesley College, and Carla Petievich of Montclair State University.

The Letters of the Urdu Alphabet

name	letter
alif	ا
be	ب
pe	پ
te	ت
Te	ٹ
se	ث
jiim	ج
ce	چ
baRii he	ح
<u>kh</u>e	خ
daal	د
Daal	ڈ
zaal	ذ
re	ر
Re	ڑ
ze	ز
<u>zh</u>e	ژ
siin	س
shiin	ش
swaad	ص

name	letter
zwaad	ض
to'e	ط
zo'e	ظ
ain	ع
ghain	غ
fe	ف
qaaf	ق
kaaf	ک
gaaf	گ
laam	ل
miim	م
nuun	ن
wao	و
choTii he	ە
do cashmii he	ھ
choTii ye	ی
baRii ye	ے

Note

The following letters represent the same sounds:

ت *(te)* and ط *(to'e)* = t   ذ *(zaal)*, ز *(ze)*, ض *(zwaad)*, and ظ *(zo'e)* = z

ث *(se)*, س *(siin)*, and ص *(swaad)* = s   ح *(baRii he)* and ە *(choTii he)* = h

2

Unit One

The Urdu script

The Urdu alphabet is based on the script that is also used to write Arabic and Persian. It consists of thirty-seven letters that represent sounds and words derived from Arabic, Persian, and several dialects of Hindi. These letters may be divided into groups depending on a common shape they share. The shapes combine semi-circles, curves, dots, and horizontal and vertical lines. In addition, the script has three short vowels, five long vowels, and two diphthongs. In contrast to the Roman or Latin alphabet, Urdu is written from right to left. It has no upper- or lowercase letters (capital or small letters). A distinctive feature of the Urdu script is that the shapes of some letters vary according to their position in a word. Thus, for example, the Urdu letter for "b" has a different shape when it is written by itself (independent form), at the beginning of a word (initial form), in the middle (medial form), or at the end (final form).

1.1 The letter "*alif*" ١ and the short vowels

The first letter of the Urdu alphabet is called "*alif*." It is a unique letter as no other letter of the alphabet has a similar shape. It is the easiest to write -- simply a vertical line ١ . The letter "*alif*" is a consonant and, like all consonants in the Urdu alphabet, it needs a vowel in order to be pronounced. Vowels in the Urdu script can be short or long. In this section we will introduce the short vowels. There are three short vowels in the script which are written as diacritics or signs above or below the consonants with which they are associated:

*short "*a*" vowel called *zabar* and indicated by placing the following sign **above** a consonant

*short "*i*" vowel called *zer* and indicated by placing the following sign **below** a consonant ِ

3

3

*short "*u*" vowel called *pesh* and indicated by placing the following sign **above** a consonant ٔ

When the letter "*alif*" is combined with these short vowels it produces the following sounds:

pronunciation	transliteration	letter
as in English "*but*" or "*must*"	a	آ
as in English "*pin*" or "*thin*"	i	اِ
as in English "*full*" or "*pull*"	u	اُ

One of the peculiarities of the Urdu, as well as Arabic and Persian alphabets, is that these short vowels are often not actually written and the reader is expected to supply them based on his or her prior knowledge of the word. The short vowels are often written only if there is a possibility of the word being misread or if the word is not commonly used, such as a word of foreign origin.

1.2 The "*be*" series

As noted, most of the letters of the Urdu alphabet can be divided into groups according to the common basic shape they share. The letters of the "*be*" series all have a basic shape similar to a long boat ب. As can be seen in the chart below, the different letters of this series are formed by adding dots above or below this shape. One letter, "*Te,*" is formed by placing a symbol resembling the English lower case "b" above the basic shape.

pronunciation	transliteration	name	letter
similar to English "b"	b	*be*	ب

similar to English "p"	p	*pe*	پ
dental t *	t	*te*	ت
palatal T **	T	*Te*	ٹ
similar to English "s"	s	*se*	ث

* pronounced with tongue against back of upper teeth

** pronounced with tongue retroflex against palate

All the letters of the "*be*" series may be combined with any of the short vowels introduced above.

Thus *"ba"* is written as بَ ; *"bi"* is written as بِ ; *"bu"* is written as بُ.

Exercise 1

Can you read these letter-vowel combinations from right to left?

پُ ثِ اَ اُ طَ بِ اُ تِ تُ طُ پِ پُ ثُ اِ تُ بَ بَ پَ طِ

Can you write the following in Urdu?

a	*i*
bi	*pu*
Tu	*si*
u	*Ti*
sa	*tu*
ti	*pa*

1.3 Unfriendly and friendly letters

There are two types of letters in the Urdu alphabet: unfriendly and friendly letters. Unfriendly letters do not connect with letters that follow them, that is, letters immediately to the left of them.

They are, therefore, also called non-connectors. The letter "*alif*" is an example of an unfriendly

letter. If it is followed by another letter it will not connect to that letter. Thus the Urdu word for

"now," "*ab*," is written as: اُب . On the other hand, friendly letters connect with letters that

follow them, that is, letters immediately to the left of them. They are, therefore, also known as

connectors. Since "friendship requires sacrifice," friendly letters will usually sacrifice a portion

of their original shape to connect to a letter to the left of them. Friendly letters, therefore, have

three forms:

*initial form at the beginning of a word

*medial form in the middle of a word

*final form at the end of a word (usually the same as the independent form)

The letters of the "*be*" series are friendly letters. In their initial and medial forms, when they

connect to a letter following them, they retain only the hook or curve at the beginning of the

letter. Any dots or signs that are part of the letter are placed above or below this truncated

portion of the letter. Here are the friendly or connecting forms of the letters of the "*be*" series:

end of word	middle of word	beginning of word	letter
ـب	ـبـ	بـ	b
ـپ	ـپـ	پـ	p
ـت	ـتـ	تـ	t
ـٹ	ـٹـ	ٹـ	T

ش   ثـ   ثـ   s

To write the word "*pab*" we need to combine the initial form of the letter "*p*" and the short "*a*"

vowel (پَ) with the letter (ب). Since the script is written from right to left, the

combination in Urdu would be written as پَب

Illustrations:

written form	components	word in transliteration
پَب	ب + پَ	*pab*
بِب	ب + بِ	*bib*
بِپَت	ب + پَ + ت	*bipat*

Exercise 2

Can you read the following letter combinations? (Most of these are random combinations and do

not represent actual words)

بُت   ثِت   اُت   ٹُپ   پَب   تِپ   ٹِپ   بِت   اِت   تُپِت   بِٹ   پِٹُت

Connect the following letters:

ث + ثِ + ث   پِ + ب

ب + ٹُ   ٹ + تُ

پ + ٹِ   ب + ثَ

ت + پِ + تَ + پِ   ث + پَ + اُ

7

1.4 The letters of the "be" series with "alif"

The letter "*alif*" is also used in Urdu to indicate a long "*aa*" vowel. This vowel is equivalent to the "*aa*" sound in "father" or "car." When combined with "*alif*," all consonants are read with this long vowel. (Note: the short "a" vowel is produced by placing a *zabar* ´ above the consonant.) Since the members of the *"be"* series are friendly, they use their initial form when joining with "*alif.*"

baa	با	ا + ب
paa	پا	ا + پ
taa	تا	ا + ت
Taa	ٹا	ا + ٹ
saa	ثا	ا + ث

1.5 Two more letters -- "*nuun*" and "*choTii ye*"

pronunciation	transliteration	name	letter
similar to English "n"	n	*nuun*	ن
similar to English "y"	y	*choTii ye*	ي

As consonants, both "*nuun*" and "*choTii ye*" ("small ye") can be combined with any of the short vowels. Thus "*nu*" is written as نُ while "*yi*" is written as يِ. They are introduced here because both are friendly letters and their beginning and middle forms have the same basic shape as that of the *"be"* series. Their final forms have the same shape as their independent forms.

end of word	middle of word	beginning of word	letter
ن	ـنـ	نـ	n
ی ⁄ ي	ـیـ	یـ	y

The following table shows the combination of these two letters with "*alif*"

naa	نا	ن + ا
yaa	یا	ی + ا

1.6 "*Alif madda*"

As we have seen above, the letter "*alif*," when combined with a consonant, functions as a long "*aa*" vowel. In a situation when we want to indicate the "*aa*" vowel sound by itself, independent of a consonant as, for example, the "*aa*" in the English word "argue," we would need to write two "*alifs*" next to each other. Since this is not orthographically permissible, we use instead a special letter -- the "*alif madda*," which is written as آ. The sign above the "*alif*," which is called the "*madda*," serves to elongate or extend the "*alif*." The "*alif madda*" usually occurs at the beginning of words.

Exercise 3

Can you read the following from right to left:

نانا بابا آپ پان بات یایا ثابا نان ٹاٹا بابا تایا ٹِنا ثُبِت

آٹ آ آت

Write out the following in the Urdu script; remember that the direction of writing is right to left:

(Remember to use "*alif madda*" آ when a word begins with a long "*aa*" vowel.)

9

Examples: taa yaa = تَايَا   paa naa = پانَا

aap	*naa yaa*
aan	*piT*
aab	*Tipu*
baa naa	*aat*
Taa paa	*baat*
taa naa	*paaT*
suT	*baa taa naa*

Unit Two

2.1 The "*jiim*" series

The letters of the "*jiim*" series share the same basic shape ﺡ ; the placement of various dots distinguishes one sound from another.

pronunciation	transliteration	name	letter
as in English "j"	j	*jiim*	ﺝ
as in English "ch"*	c	*ce*	ﺝ
as in English "h"	h	*baRii he*	ﺡ
voiceless fricative**	kh	*khe*	ﺥ

*as "ch" in "church"

** similar to "ch" in Scottish "loch" or German "ach"

The letter ﺡ ("*baRii he*" or "big h") is one of two "h"s in Urdu, both of which are pronounced in exactly the same way. The "*baRii he*" occurs only in words of Arabic origin and, therefore, occurs less frequently than the other "h" *("choTii he*" or "small h"), which we will learn later. The letter ﺥ (kh) is found only in words borrowed from Arabic or Persian. The letters of the "*jiim*" series are friendly, connecting with letters that follow them. The table below illustrates their initial, medial, and final forms.

end of word	middle of word	beginning of word	letter
ﺞ	ﺠ	ﺟ	j
ﭻ	ﭽ	ﭼ	c
ﺢ	ﺤ	ﺣ	h

11

خ   خ‍   ‍خ   <u>kh</u>

Illustrations:

written form	components	word in transliteration
جَب	جَ + ب	*jab*
بَحَث	بَ + حَ + ث	*bahas*
جَج	جَ + ج	*jaj*
نِجات	نِ + ج + ا + ت	*nijaat*
چَخان	چَ + خ + ا + ن	*ca<u>kh</u>aan*

Exercise 1

Can you read the following letter combinations?

چُپ   بِت   چاپ   پُکَت   تَخَ   نَج   نُج   حُب   بَحَث   بَچَن   تَخَت   بَچَن

Can you write the following letter combinations in Urdu?

jab   cipat

ba<u>kh</u>   jacan

hijas   haTij

bic   cu<u>kh</u>an

taaj   puj

yucun   niT

2.2 Letters of the "*jiim*" series with "*alif*"

Since the letters of the "*jiim*" series are friendly, they use their initial forms when joining with the "*alif*":

jaa	جا	ج + ا
caa	چا	چ + ا
haa	حا	ح + ا
<u>kh</u>aa	خا	خ + ا

Exercise 2

Can you read the following letter combinations from right to left?

ناجا   آجا حاپا   آپا   ثاچا چایا ثانا خاجا حاجا پاچا ٹاجا تاحا خاتا

Combine the following letters to create the words indicated in parentheses (remember that "*alif*" is not a friendly letter and will not connect to any letters following it):

(banaanaa) ا+ ن + ا + ن+بَ   (paajaa) ا+ ج + ا+ پ

(taajaa) ا+ ج+ ا+ ت   (haayaa) ح +ا + ي + ا

(jaapiT) ٹ + پِ + ا + ج   (<u>kh</u>aanaa) خ+ ا+ ن + ا

(naasi<u>kh</u>) خ+ شِ + ا + ن   (aab) ب+ ا+ ا

(hijaab) ب +ا + ج + حِ   (caacaa) چَ+ا+ چ + ا

13

2.3 "ChoTii ye" as "ii" vowel

In addition to functioning as the consonant "y," the "choTii ye" (or "small y"), when combined with consonants, serves to indicate the long "ii" vowel. This vowel gives the "ii" sound in English words such as "feel," "seal," "peal." The following table shows the forms of the various consonants we have learned so far when combined with a "choTii ye." Note that it is not necessary to place the two dots beneath the "choTii ye" when it occurs at the end of a word.

bii	بی	ب + ی
pii	پی	پ + ی
tii	تی	ت + ی
Tii	ٹی	ٹ + ی
sii	ثی	ث + ی
nii	نی	ن + ی
yii	یی	ی + ی
jii	جی	ج + ی
cii	چی	چ + ی
hii	حی	ح + ی
khii	خی	خ + ی

Exercise 3

The following words each contain letters in two clusters. Can you read them from right to left?

جی‌جی   بی‌بی   حاجی   ناچی   ٹی‌پی   آپا   تی‌نی   اخی   چابی   پاپی

Can you write the following word clusters in the Urdu script? For the purposes of this exercise,

14

if the first cluster ends in *"choTii ye,"* do not connect it with letters that follow it.

(jii jaa) ا+ ج ي + ج

(sii baa) ا + ب + ي + ث

(sii taa) ا+ ت + ي + ث

(jaa nii) ج ا+ ن ي+

(yaa nii) ي ا + ن ي+

(cii nii) چ ي + ن ي+

(paa nii) پ ا+ ن ي+

(naa nii) ن ا+ ن ي +

(jaapaanii) ج +ا+ پ+ ا+ ن+ ي

(Tii bii) ٹ + ب + ي+ ي

2.4 The letter *"wao"* or *"vav"* as a consonant

The letter و *"wao"* or *"vav"* functions both as a consonant as well as a vowel. When it occurs at the beginning of words it functions as a consonant. As a consonant it represents the sound "v" as in the English "vacation" and "vacancy." Since many speakers in the subcontinent do not differentiate between the English "v" and "w," this consonant is sometimes also pronounced as "w." The letter و is an unfriendly letter so it does not connect to any letters that follow it (i.e., to the left), and consequently, it retains the same shape regardless of whether it is at the beginning, middle, or end of a word.

Illustrations:

written form	components	word in transliteration
وات	و + ا+ ت	*vaat*
واجِب	و + ا + جِ + ب	*vaajib*

وِ + پ + ا + ٹ   وِپاٹ   *vipaaT*

ب + ا + و + ا   باوا   *baavaa*

Reminder: in the above examples neither the *"wao"* nor the *"alif"* connects with letters that follow them since they are unfriendly.

Exercise 4

Can you read the following?

واچ   وان   تاوان   پاوا   وات   واجی   بی وی   واچن   واِجب   واِجبات

واپی

Can you write the words below in the Urdu script? Do not connect words written in two clusters

vii Tii	*vijan*
baavii	*vaa caa*
caa van	*viyaap*
sii vaa	*khaavii*
sivaat	*vubit*

2.5 The letter *"wao"* as a vowel

In addition to being a consonant, the letter و also represents one of the following vowel sounds:

* the long vowel *"uu,"* as in the English "rude," "shrewd," or "food"

* the vowel *"o,"* as in English "more," "four," or "torment"

* the diphthong *"au,"* as in English "moat" or "coat"

Thus the word جو (و+ج) could be read as *"juu," "jo,"* or *"jau."* The following conventions may be used to distinguish between the three sounds associated with *"vao"*:

* the *"uu"* vowel by the *pesh* ' sign above the *"wao,"* or the consonant to which it is

attached, e.g., *juu* = جُو .

* the *"o"* vowel remains unmarked.

* the diphthong *"au"* by the *zabar* ´ above the *"wao,"* or the consonant to which it is attached,

e.g., *jau* = جَو .

In most writing, however, the use of these superscript signs is restricted to the unusual

circumstance of new or rare words. Otherwise, these signs are omitted, and only context and

prior knowledge of the word help the reader determine which one of the three readings is

correct.

The table below illustrates the consonants we have learned so far combined with *"wao"* vowel.

buu, bo, bau	بو	ب + و
puu, po, pau	پو	پ + و
tuu, to, tau	تو	ت + و
Tuu, To, Tau	ٹو	ٹ + و
suu, so, sau	ثو	ث + و
nuu, no, nau	نو	ن + و
yuu, yo, yau	یو	ی + و
juu, jo, jau	جو	ج + و
cuu, co, cau	چو	چ + و

17

huu, ho, hau	حو	ح + و
khuu, kho, khau	خو	خ + و
vuu, vo, vau	وو	و + و*

<u>Note:</u>

* The first "_wao_" functions here as the consonant "v" or "w."

Remember that any word beginning with a short "u" vowel must begin with اُ just as any word that has a short "i" vowel in the beginning must commence with اِ (see unit 1).

Exercise 5

Can you read the following from right to left? (The "_wao_" may be read as any one of the three vovel sounds "_uu_," "_o_," or "_au_," depending on vowel marking; if there is no specific marking, read as "_o_.")

جوجو بابو چوُچو یویو خوُخی توُتی پوٹی خوُن جوُتا ٹوُٹا

خوُنی بو پوُجا پاٹ ناوُناوُ پوتا چوپیٹ خاتوُن

Can you write the following words in Urdu?

bobii	_job_
buubuu	_caubaa_
ponii	_juuhuu_
Topii	_soho_
Tonii	_nono_
khuub	_caupaan_

18

Unit Three

3.1 *"BaRii ye"* as a vowel

The *"baRii ye"* or "big y" ﮮ represents two vowel sounds:

* the *"e"* vowel similar to the sound *"e"* in English "check"

* the diphthong *"ai"* similar to the sound *"ai"* in English "pain"

The following table illustrates the *"baRii ye"* combined with various consonants:

be, bai	بﮯ	ﮮ + بِ
pe, pai	پﮯ	ﮮ + پِ
te, tai	تﮯ	ﮮ + تِ
Te, Tai	ٹﮯ	ﮮ + ٹ
se, sai	ثﮯ	ﮮ + ثِ
ne, nai	نﮯ	ﮮ + ن
ve, vai	وﮯ	ﮮ + و
je, jai	جﮯ	ﮮ + جِ
ce, cai	چﮯ	ﮮ + چ
he, hai	حﮯ	ﮮ + حِ
<u>*kh*</u>*e,* <u>*kh*</u>*ai*	خﮯ	ﮮ + خ

To differentiate the *"e"* vowel from the *"ai"* vowel, the superscript sign *zabar* ´ is placed

above the vowel or the consonant to which it is attached. This indicates that the vowel is to be

read as *"ai."* For example بﮯ would be read as *"bai."* In everyday writing and printing,

however, the *zabar* is rarely indicated, leaving the choice of reading the *"baRii ye"* as *"e"* or

19

"*ai*" to the reader's prior familiarity with the word and context.

Exercise 1

Can you read the word clusters below? ("*BaRii ye*" may be read either as "*e*" or "*ai*" unless

indicated otherwise):

وی تے   ثے ثے   ٹی ٹے   یے چے   خے تے   بے بے

پا پے   جا جے   نے چا   حا تی   آ خے   جے پی

Write the following word clusters in Urdu script:

bii bai	*pe paa*
pe ye	*je je*
se jau	*hai hai*
bii je pii	*khe nai*
Taa te	*aa be*
ce hii	*he To*
khuu jai	*cai cii*

3.2 Medial forms of "*choTii ye*" and "*baRii ye*"

"*ChoTii ye*" and "*baRii ye*" are friendly letters, connecting to letters that may follow them.

Both, however, have the same form in the middle of words: ﻴ   Between consonants,

therefore, this medial form may represent either "*ii*" ("*choTii ye*") or "*e*" or "*ai*" ("*baRii ye*").

The following superscript and subscript markings are used to distinguish among the three

possible readings of the medial forms, although in common practice these signs are not

frequently used and the reader is expected to provide the correct vowel from context.

* medial form of "*choTii ye*" marked by a *zer* ِ placed below the letter

* medial form of "*baRii ye*" to indicate the "*e*" vowel remains unmarked

* medial form of "*baRii ye*" to indicate the "*ai*" vowel marked by a *zabar* َ placed above the

letter

Illustrations:

biit	بیِت	ب + یِ + ت
bet	بیت	ب + ے + ت
bait	بیَت	ب + ے + ت

Exercise 2

Can you read the following from right to left?

چِین   چِینی   ثِیاب   چِتا   نَین   پیٹ   پیِت   نَیح   بیچا

Combine the following letters, which include medial forms of "*choTii ye*" and "*baRii ye*," to

create the words indicated in parentheses:

ت + یِ + ن (tiin)	ح + ے + ش (hais)
چ + ے + ن (cain)	چ + یِ + ن (ciin)
ب + ے + ٹ + یِ (beTii)	ط + یِ + ب + ا (Tiibaa)
پ + یِ + ن (piin)	ب + یِ + ج + نَ (najiib)
ب + ے + ن (bain)	ت + ے + ج + یِ (tejii)

21

و + يِ + چ (viic)   جْ + ـے + ب (jeb)

3.3 The letters "kaaf," "gaaf," and "laam"

The shapes of these three letters have, as a common feature, a vertical line slightly curved to the

left at the bottom. In the case of "kaaf," a leftward slanting line is connected to the top of this

line. For the "gaaf," two such parallel lines are added.

pronunciation	transliteration	name	letter
similar to English "k"	k	kaaf	ک
similar to English "g"	g	gaaf	گ
similar to English "l"	l	laam	ل

All three letters are friendly, connecting to letters to their left. On account of the vertical line in

their basic shape, they have special forms when combining with "alif":

end of word	middle of word	beginning of word	with "alif"**	letter
سک	سکب	کب	کا	k
سگ	سگب	گب	گا	g
سل	سلب*	لب*	لا	l

Note:

*Although the initial and medial forms of the letter "laam" resemble those of "alif," they, unlike

the "alif," connect with the letter that follows. Thus, کب would read as "lab" while اَب

would read as "ab."

**"Kaaf" and "gaaf," when combining with "laam," use the same initial shape as they do with

22

"alif":

کل   ک + ل

گل   گ + ل

The following table illustrates the forms of these letters with various long vowels:

pronunciation	with "*vao*"	pronunciation	with "*baRii ye*"	pronunciation	with "*choTii ye*"	letter
kuu, ko, kau	کو	*ke, kai*	کے	*kii*	کی	ک
guu, go, gau	گو	*ge, gai*	گے	*gii*	گی	گ
luu, lo, lau	لو	*le, lai*	لے	*lii*	لی	ل

Illustrations:

written form	components	word in transliteration
کالا	ک + ا + ل + ا	*kaalaa*
لیگا	ل + ے + گ + ا	*legaa*
لوح	ح + و + ل	*lauh*
گلاب	گ + ل + ا + ب	*gulaab*

Exercise 3

Combine the following letters to form the word given in transliteration. Be sure to distinguish

between friendly and unfriendly letters.

ک + ا + پ + ی (*kaapii*)   ل + جَ + ا (*lajaa*)

گ + ا + ن + ا (*gaanaa*)   ل + و + گ (*log*)

23

چ + ا + ک +و (caakuu)   گ + ي+ت (giit)

ن+ے+ک (nek)   بِ + گ + ا+ن + ا (bigaanaa)

خ + ي+ک + ا (khaakii)   ٹ + ي + ک + ا (Tiikaa)

Can you read the words below?

کاکی   لالا   خالی   کِتاب   گول   جُگ   بَلا   بُلبُل   بوُک

لوٹ   لِیگ   کوٹن   کباب   ثالِث   کوؤلی   چولی   لیٹ   چال   چَلَن

Write the following in the Urdu script?

laulaak	lekin	naalaa
lonaa	kaabul	taalaa caabii
laukik	gup cup	jogan
kaajal	gopaal	gaajan
lagaan	log	baabul

3.4 Independent forms of vowels

When a vowel is the initial sound in a word, as in the English word "of" or the Urdu word "aaj," the letter "alif" is used as the carrier for the vowel. The following table illustrates the possible options:

independent form	vowel
اَ	a
اِ	i

24

اُ	*u*
آ	*aa*
اِي*	*ii*
اوُ	*uu*
اے*	*e*
اَے*	*ai*
او	*o*
اَو	*au*

* Since "*choTii ye*" and "*baRii ye*" are friendly letters, they will assume their medial form if they are followed by another consonant. For example: "*ek*" (اے + ک) is written as ایک.

Illustrations:

written form	components	word in transliteration
آواتی	آ + و + ا + ت + ي	*aavaatii*
ایکا	ا + ک + اے + ا	*ekaa*
این	ن + اَے + ا	*ain*

Exercise 4

Can you read these words?

اوج آنا اَلپ اَگیلا اِٹیکیٹ اَنیک آگے ایکٹا اِچ ایل اِل

25

Write the words below in the Urdu script?

ulTaa	*aaj*
aayaat	*en (Anne)*
aayaa	*in*
ovan (oven)	*oTaa*
avical	*on*
eg (egg)	*aaluu*

Unit Four

4.1 The "*daal*" series

The letters of the "*daal*" series share a common shape: د. The difference between this shape and that of "*wao*" و should be carefully noted: the top of "*wao*" is rounded into a small circle. The the letters of the "*daal*" series are:

pronunciation	transliteration	name	letter
dental d*	d	*daal*	د
palatal D**	D	*Daal*	ڈ
as in English "z"***	z	*zaal*	ذ

*softer than the English "d"; pronounced with tongue placed against the back of the upper teeth

**pronounced with tongue retroflex against palate; similar to English "d" as in "dog"

***identical in pronunciation to "*ze*" (introduced below); occurs only in Arabic words

The letters of the "*daal*" series are unfriendly and, therefore, do not connect with letters that follow them. Consequently, there are no differences in their initial, medial, and final shapes. The table below illustrates their combinations with various long vowels:

pronunciation	with "*wao*"	pronunciation	with "*baRii ye*"	pronunciation	with "*choTii ye*"	letter
duu, do, dau	دو	de, dai	دے	dii	دی	د
Duu, Do, Dau	ڈو	De, Dai	ڈے	Dii	ڈی	ڈ
zuu, zo, zau	ذو	ze, zai	ذے	zii	ذی	ذ

27

Illustrations:

written form	components	word in transliteration
دال	د + ا + ل	daal
جَدِید	جَ + د + ي + د	jadiid
ڈُوبَن	ڈ + و + بَ + ن	Duuban
ذُنُوب	ذُ + ن + و + ب	zunuub
ذَبِیح	ذَ + ب + ي + ح	zabiih

Exercise 1

Read the words below:

دادا   ڈیڈی   دیدی   ڈاک   آدو   وادی   ذات   دیٹ   کاذِب

جُدا   دِل   والے

Combine the following letters to form the words given in parentheses (remember that letters of

the "*daal*" series are unfriendly):

حُ + د + و + د (huduud)   حَ + د + ي + ث (hadiis)

جَ + ا + ذِ + ب (jaazib)   تَ + ا + د + ي + ب (taadiib)

ڈ + ا + کِ + ن (Daakin)   ذَ + و + ا + نِ + ب (zawaanib)

ڈَ + بَ + ل (Dabal)   ڈ + و + ل + ا (Dolaa)

ڈ + ا + ک + و + ا + ل + ا (Daak waalaa)   د + و + ل + ت (daulat)

28

ُث + و + د + ح (huduus)   ي + ن + ا + و + ي + د (diivaanii)

Can you write these words in Urdu?

Daalaa	*biidii*
jaaduu	*zawii*
Dapol	*<u>kh</u>udaa*
paDaa	*deg*
diipak	*de do*

4.2 The "*re*" series

The letters of the "*re*" series share a common shape: ر. It is often difficult for beginners to distinguish this shape from that of the "*daal*" series د. The "*re*" shape has more of a slant in its stroke (an angle greater than 90 degrees). The "*daal*" shape, in contrast, makes a smaller angle (less than 90 degrees) and has a slight curve in the middle. The following are the letters of this series:

pronunciation	transliteration	name	letter
as in English "r"	r	*re*	ر
retroflexive R *	R	*Re*	ڑ
as in English "z"**	z	*ze*	ز
alveopalatal fricative***	<u>zh</u>	*<u>zh</u>e*	ژ

* pronounced with tongue retroflex against palate (roof of mouth) and then flapped forward; never occurs at the beginning of a word

**the most common transcription of "z" sound in Urdu; occurs more frequently than "*zaal*" introduced above

***pronunciation similar to "s" in the English words "pleasure" and "vision"; occurs very rarely

29

Like the letters of the "*daal*" series, the letters of the "*re*" series are unfriendly. The table below

illustrates the combination of the "*re*" series with vowels:

pronunciation	with "*wao*"	pronunciation	with "*baRii ye*"	pronunciation	with "*choTii ye*"	letter
ruu, ro, rau	رو	re, rai	رے	rii	ری	ر
Ruu, Ro, Rau	ڑو	Re, Rai	ڑے	Rii	ڑی	ڑ
zuu, zo, zau	زو	ze, zai	زے	zii	زی	ز
<u>zh</u>uu, <u>zh</u>o, <u>zh</u>au	ژو	<u>zh</u>e, <u>zh</u>ai	ژے	<u>zh</u>ii	ژی	ژ

Illustrations:

written form	components	word in transliteration
ریت	ر + ے + ت	*ret*
توڑا	ت + و + ڑ + ا	*toRaa*
ژاژ	ژ + ا + ژ	*<u>zh</u>aa<u>zh</u>*
بازار	ب + ا + ز + ا + ر	*baazaar*

Exercise 2

Can you read the words below?

ٹاڑا   راجا   رانی   روڈ   لاری   یاری   گاڑی   پارٹی   آزادی

گڑبڑ   ژالا   پُرانا   روبَرٹ   راجا کی رانی

Combine the following letters to form the words indicated in parentheses (remember, letters of

the "*re*" series are unfriendly):

(zhuliidaa) ژ + و + ل + ي + د + ا   (khizaan) خِ + ز + ا + ن

ب + ر + ب + ا + د + ي (bar baadii)   ز + ے + وَ + ر (zevar)

کِ + چَ + ڑ (kicaR)   ٹ + و + ڑ + ي (ToRii)

پ + ے + ز + ا + ر (paizaar)   ر + ے + ح + ا + ن (raihaan)

ثُ + ر + ے + ا (suraiyaa)   ج + و + ڑ + ن (joRan)

Can you write these words in Urdu? (use "*ze*" for "z")

baRii	*piiRaa*
raajẕu	*zor*
khariid	*jaaRaa*
zaade	*tajaavuuz*
roTii	*zhiyaan*
teraa jaaduu cal gayaa	*diivaar*

4.3 The letter "*miim*"

The letter "*miim*" represents the sound equivalent to "m" in English. It is a friendly letter and adopts these forms when at the beginning, middle, and end of words:

end of word	middle of word	beginning of word	independent form	letter
مؕ	ـمـ	مـ	م	m

The following chart shows the combination of "*miim*" with various vowels:

with "*wao*"	with "*baRii ye*"	with "*choTii ye*"	with "*alif*"
مو	مے	می	ما

31

Illustrations:

written form	components	word in transliteration
موتی	م + و + ٹ + ی	*moTii*
خَمر	خ + مَ + ر	*khamar*
مَرَم	مَ + رَ + م	*maram*
مَدَد	مَ + دَ + د	*madad*
کام	ک + ا + م	*kaam*

Exercise 3

Read the words below:

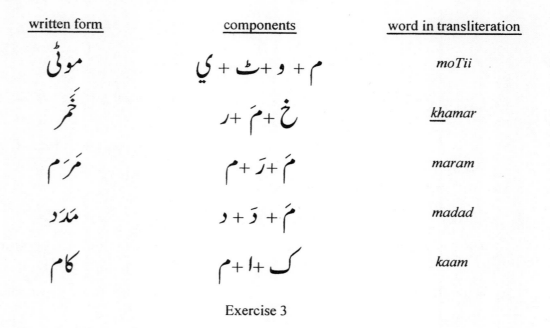

مامی   رام   ماپ   بَرما   مَکان   آم   ٹِم   ٹڈونا

حَمید   رومیو   ٹام   لمبا   گملا   گمرا

Combine the following letters to create words indicated in parentheses:

اِ + م + ک + ا + ن (imkaan)   م + ے + ڈَ + م (meDam)

م + ا + رَ + گ (maarag)   مَ + رِ + ی + ا (mariyaa)

جَ + م + ا + ل (jamaal)   زُ + ک + ا + م (zukaam)

ثَ + مَ + ر (samar)   خَ + مَ + ر (khamar)

ٹِ + م + ا + ک (Timaak)   چَ + مَ + ن (caman)

32

Can you write these words in Urdu?

zamiin	mujaavir
haraam	kamiin
<u>kh</u>umaar	camak
TamaaTar	balam
Dom	aalaam

4.4 The "hamza" at vowel junctions

The "hamza" is an orthographic sign resembling the number "2" written in reverse and slightly above the line: ٔ . The "hamza" is used in Urdu to separate two vowels when they occur next to each other without any intervening consonants. Such is the case, for example, in the Urdu word "aao" ("come") where the "aa" vowel is next to the "o" vowel, or in the word "koii" where the "o" vowel occurs before the "ii" vowel. The following rules are observed in the placement of the "hamza" with specific vowels:

If the second vowel is indicated by the letter "wao" (i.e. "uu", "o" or "au") then the "hamza" is written directly above the "wao." Examples:

written form	components	word in transliteration
آؤ	و + آ	aao
لاؤ	و + ا + ل	laaoo

If the second vowel is a short "i" vowel or indicated by "choTii ye" (i.e. "ii"), then it is necessary to have a small hook before it (the second vowel). This hook, which resembles the medial form of the "be" series, becomes the "chair" or "kursii" for the "hamza." Note: a "kursii" is not necessary before a *"baRii ye"* at the end of a word.

Examples:

written form	components	word in transliteration
کوئی	ک + و +ی	*koii*
گائے	گ + ا + ے	*gaae*
پِئے	پِ + ے	*piee*
نائٹ	ن + ا + اِ + ٹ	*naaiT*

Note: There are several vowel combinations -- *"iiaa," "iie," "iio"* -- in which the *"hamza"* is not

usually employed.

Exercise 4

Can you read the words below?

نائی   پائی   چائے   روئے   مائی   وائیٹ   ڈارلِنگ   وائین

چائینیز   مائیکل   کائیٹ   ٹائیپ رائیٹر   "آئی لو یو!"

Combine the following letters to form the words indicated in parentheses (remember to use a

"hamza" in between vowels with no intervening consonants):

(jaaoo) ج +ا + ء+ و   *(raae)* ر +ا + ء+ ے

(milaae) مِ +ل+ ا + ء+ ے   *(bataaii)* بَ +ت +ا + ء+ ی

(judaaii) جُ + د+ا + ء+ ی   *(pilaao)* پِ +ل+ ا + ء+ و

گ + ا + ۓ + ی (gaaii)   گَ + ۓ + ی (gaii)

Write these words in Urdu:

laaiin   jagaao

calaae   paao

Taaii   Taaiim

malaaii   naaiiT aauuT

Unit Five

5.1 The letters "*fe*" and "*qaaf*"

The letters "*fe*" and "*qaaf*" share a common element: a closed loop or circle at the top of the letter, similar to that found in "*wao*." However, "*fe*" has one dot over this loop while "*qaaf*" has two. In addition, as the chart below illustrates, the two letters differ in the shape of their respective independent forms: the shape of "*fe*" resembles the "*be*" series while that of "*qaaf*" is similar to that of "*nuun*," or the letter "n."

pronunciation	transliteration	name	letter
similar to English "f"	f	*fe*	ف
voiceless back-velar stop*	q	*qaaf*	ق

* similar to English "k" but pronounced further back in the throat.

Both letters are friendly, retaining only the loop with superscript dot/s, in their initial and medial forms:

end of word	middle of word	beginning of word	independent form	letter
ـف	ـفـ	فـ	ف	f
ـق	ـقـ	قـ	ق	q

The table shows the combination of these letters with various vowels:

with "*wao*"	with "*baRii ye*"	with "*choTii ye*"	with "*alif*"
فو	ـفے	فی	فا
قو	ـقے	قی	قا

36

Illustrations:

written form	components	word in transliteration
فوج	ف + و + ج	*fauj*
قریب	ق + ر + ی + ب	*qariib*
کافی	ک + ا + ف + ی	*kaafii*
حقیقت	ح + ق + ی + ق + ت	*haqiiqat*
قاف	ق + ا + ف	*qaaf*

Exercise 1

Can you read these words?

باقی   بَقا   فوفو   فانی   قَید   فقیر   قُفل   مَفروح   حُرَف

مَفلوک   قُفل   قانون   فَریق   بَرَف   چاقو   حَلَق   رِزائی

فوٹوگراف   فری ورلڈ   مَفلر   کِلفٹن

Combine the following letters to create words indicated in parentheses:

(maqaam) مَ + ق + ا + م   (kafan) کَ + فَ + ن

(qamar) قَ + مَ + ر   (firoz) فِ + ر + و + ز

(fareb) فَ + ر + ے + ب   (qaabil) ق + ا + ب + ل

(mufiid) مُ + ف + ی + د   (taaliif) ت + ا + ل + ی + ف

37

آ + فِ + ر + ي + ن (afiriin)   اِ + ف + ا + قَ + ت (ifaaqat)

Can you write these words in Urdu?

fon   aafaaq

foTo   qaatil

zauq (use "zaal" for "z")   qaaed

khafaa   varaq

qalam   friiDam

5.2 "ChoTii he"

"ChoTii he" is one of two letters for the "h" sound in Urdu. The other, as we have already

learned, is "baRii he" (ح). Of the two, "choTii he" occurs more frequently since the use of

"baRii he" is limited to a few words of Arabic origin. "ChoTii he" is the most idiosyncratic letter

in the Urdu script since its initial, medial, and final forms are not predictable. Its initial and

medial form consists of a slight "dip" below the line with a small hook underneath while its final

form (when preceded by a friendly letter) is a horizontal line with a small drop at the end. The

various forms of "choTii he" are shown below:

final*	medial	initial	pronunciation	transliteration	name	letter
ــہ	ہ	ہ	h*	h	choTii he	ہ

*the final form varies according to whether the "choTii he" is preceded by a friendly or unfriendly letter. After
unfriendly letters, "choTii he" adopts its independent form.

* for pronunciation of "choTii he" at the end of a word, see below

One of the peculiarities of "choTii he" is the special form that it adopts at the beginning of a

word when it joins an "alif." It uses the initial/medial form of the "be" series with a hook underneath. On the other hand, when "*choTii he*" joins an "*alif*" in the middle of a word it adopts its regular medial form. The table below shows "*choTii he*" combined with the various vowels:

with "*wao*"	with "*baRii ye*"	with "*choTii ye*"	with "*alif*" (medial)	with "*alif*" (initial)
ہو	ہے	ہی	ہا	ہا

Illustrations:

written form	components	word in transliteration
ہوتا	ا + ت + و + ہ	hotaa
ہار	ہ + ا + ر	haar
بہار	بَ + ہ + ا + ر	bahaar
جگہ	جَ + گَ + ہ	jagah
لوہو	ل + و + ہ + و	lohuu

Exercise 2

Can you read these words?

ہائی ہوئے ہَرمِزی ہیرا آہ راہ چاہا ہاہا

ہَرپ ہَکلاپن ہَوائی پَہاڑ دَہَن جَہان گوہر لاہور ہزار

Combine the following letters to form the words indicated in parentheses:

(hamaare) ہ + م + ا + ر + ے

(paahunaaii) پ + ا + ہُ + ن + اُ + ء + ا + ی

(jawaahir) جَ + و + اِ + ہ + ر

(qaahir) ق + ا + ہِ + ر

39

(gaahak) گ +ا + ۀ+ ک   (caahat) چ +ا + ۀ+ ت

(raahii) ر +ا + ۀ+ ی   (halaak) ۀ +ل +ا + ک

(hataadar) ۀ +ت +ا + دَ+ ر   (paahal) پ +ا + ۀ+ ل

Write these words in the Urdu script:

haadii	caaho
hoTel	jahaan
hom	haaruun
holii	fahiim
cuuhaa	gahan
kohaanaa	aagaahii

5.3 *"ChoTii he"* and pronunciation

"ChoTii he" is an idiosyncratic letter not only because of its irregular forms but also because of

the unusual pronunciation that is associated with it. In this regard, there are two situations which

should be noted:

1) *"ChoTii he"* at the end of words

In many words, a final *"choTii he"* in a word is not pronounced, often serving to elongate the

short vowel of the letter that immediately precedes it. For example: خرابہ is pronounced as

"*kharaabaa*" rather than "*kharaabah*"; راجہ "*raajaa*" instead of "*raajah*."

In a few cases, a final *"choTii he"* may be pronounced as a short vowel. For example: کہ

pronounced as "*ke*" or "*ki*" while **وہ** is read as "*vo(h)*."

2) *"ChoTii he"* in the middle of words

"*ChoTii he*" (and "*baRii he*") in the middle of a word may affect the pronunciation of a preceding short vowel in the following ways:

A preceding "*zabar*," or short "*a*" vowel, will change its pronunciation to a short "*e*." For example, the word کہنا "*kahanaa*" will be pronounced as "*kehnaa*" -- the "*a*" vowel preceding "*choTii he*" will be pronounced as "*e*." (In this particular word, the second short "*a*" vowel between "h" and "n" is also omitted in pronunciation. For an explanation see unit 7.)

A preceding "*zer*" or short "*i*" vowel will be pronounced as a short "*e*." For example: مہربانی "*mihrbaanii*" will be pronounced "*mehrbaanii*."

A preceding "*pesh*" or short "*u*" vowel will be pronounced as a short "*o*." For example: تحفہ "*tuhfah*" will be pronounced "*tohfa*."

<u>Note</u>: The Urdu script does not have signs to depict a short "*e*" or short "*o*" vowel. The "*baRii ye*" and "*wao*" are used to represent only the long "*e*" and "*o*" vowels.

Exercise 3

Read the words below. Be sure to pay attention to any peculiarities that may occur in pronunciation because of the presence of "*choTii he*" or "*baRii he*" in the middle of the word:

محفِل   اِرادہ   رَحمت   زَہر   یہ   وہ   آلوُچہ   زیادہ   وَجہ   پاجامہ

تازہ   بَہُت   خَزانہ   نُمیرہ   پہلی   خریدہ   ٹیکہ   کمینہ

5.4 *"Do cashmii he"* and aspiration

The "*do cashmii he*" or "h with the two eyes" is used in Urdu to indicate aspirated consonants.

Aspirated consonants are produced by aspirating or expelling a puff of air from the mouth while pronouncing them. A good test of whether a letter is being aspirated or not is to place your hand in front of your mouth while pronouncing the letter; if you feel a burst of air as you pronounce the letter, then aspiration is present. To write an aspirated consonant in the Urdu script a "*do cashmii he*" (ﮪ) is added to a consonant. An aspirated consonant is commonly transliterated in the English alphabet by adding an "h" to the original consonant (the aspirated form of "b," for example, would be transliterated as "bh"). Note, however, that in Urdu a consonant combined with "*do cashmii he*," for example, "bh" (ھ.), functions as a single aspirated letter. The aspirated consonant can be combined with any vowels. Thus بھا would be read as "*bhaa*;" بھی as "*bhii*," etc. "*Do cashmii he*" is a friendly letter and there is very little variation in its independent, initial, medial, and final forms. The following table shows the major aspirated consonants and their combinations with the various vowels:

with "wao"	"with *baRii ye*"	"with *choTii ye*"	with "*alif*"	aspirated form	consonant
(bhuu, bho, bha) بھو	(bhe, bhai) بھے	(bhii) بھی	(bhaa) بھا	(bh) ھ.	(b) ب
پھو	پھے	پھی	پھا	(ph) پھ	(p) پ
تھو	تھے	تھی	تھا	(th) تھ	(t) ت
ٹھو	ٹھے	ٹھی	ٹھا	(Th) ٹھ	(T) ٹ
جھو	جھے	جھی	جھا	(jh) جھ	(j) ج
چھو	چھے	چھی	چھا	(ch) چھ	(c) چ
دھو	دھے	دھی	دھا	(dh) دھ	(d) د
ڈھو	ڈھے	ڈھی	ڈھا	(Dh) ڈھ	(D) ڈ
ڑھو	ڑھے	ڑھی	ڑھا	*(Rh) ڑھ	*(R) ڑ

کھو	کھے	کھی	کھا	(kh) کھ	(k) ک
گھو	گھے	گھی	گھا	(gh) گھ	(g) گ

* Never occurs at the beginning of words.

Aspirations often make a crucial difference in the meaning of Urdu words. The presence or absence of aspiration with a consonant may change the entire meaning of a word. For instance, "*baap*" (باپ) is "father," but "*bhaap*" (بھاپ) is "steam"; "*kaal*" (کال) is "famine," while "*khaal*" (کھال) is "a hide, skin."

Illustrations:

written form	components	word in transliteration
کھانا	کھ + ا + ن + ا	khaanaa
پڑھے	پَ + ڑھ + ے	paRhe
پیٹھ	پ + ی + ٹھ	piiTh
بُدھ	بُ + دھ	budh
گھڑی	گھَ + ڑ + ی	ghaRii

Exercise 4

Read the words below:

گھوڑا ڈھائی بھائی بوڑھا بھابھی گبھی ٹھِکانہ ڈھیر پَڑھائی

پھَل تھالی دھرمیندَر آڑھَت جُھمکا ماتھورا مدھومالتی پھول

کِھلے ٹھُمری ڈھولکی

43

Combine the following letters to form words indicated in parentheses:

(haath) تھ + ا + ه   (jhuumar) ر + مَ + و + جھ

(chaaliyaa) ا + ي + لِ + ا + چھ   (ghaaT) ٹ + ا + گھ

(TeRhaa) ا + ڑھ + ے + ٹ   (Dhaaii) ي + ء + ا + ڈھ

(phiTaanaa) ا + ن + ا + ٹ + پھِ   (duudh) دھ + و + د

(khet) ت + ے + کھ   (Thaakur) ر + کُ + ا + ٹھ

Can you write these words in Urdu?

aadhii   miThaaii

bhaauu   chaRii

Thiik   chuurii

mathuuraa   magar mach

jhaaRuu   phuupaa

phandaa   madhubaalaa

Dholak   rekhaa

44

Unit Six

6.1 The "*siin*" series

The *"siin"* series consists of two sibilants, "*siin*" and "*shiin,*" corresponding to the sounds "s" and "sh." "*Siin*" is the letter most commonly used to indicate the "s" sound in Urdu; the letters "*se,*" (which we have already learned) and "*swaad*" (introduced below) are also used to represent "s" but they occur less frequently than "*siin*" since they are found only in certain words of Arabic origin. The letters in the "*siin*" series may be written in two alternate ways: (a) a horizontal line indented with three "teeth" which descends into a curve: س; or (b) an unindented slightly curved horizontal line descending into a curve: س . Both forms are used interchangeably, even within the same word or sentence. In this text we will be using the indented form. "*Shiin*" is distinguished from "*siin*" by the three dots above it. "*Siin*" and "*shiin*" are friendly letters. The table below illustrates their initial, medial, and final forms (note: both indented and unindented forms are shown):

end of word	middle of word	beginning of word	independent form	letter
س	ـسـ	سـ	س	S (*siin*)
				(indented form)
س	ـسـ	سـ	س	S (*siin*)
				(unindented form)
ش	ـشـ	شـ	ش	sh (*shiin*)
				(indented form)

45

ش   شـ   ـشـ   ـش   **sh** *(shiin)*

(unindented form)

The following chart illustrates the combination of "*siin*" and "*shiin*" with long vowels:

with "*wao*"	with"*baRii ye*"	with "*choTii ye*"	with "*alif*" (medial)	letter
سو	سے	سی	سا	س
سو	سے	سی	سا	س
شو	شے	شی	شا	ش
شو	شے	شی	شا	ش

The chart below shows the combination of *"siin"* and *"shiin"* with letters of other shapes that

commonly pose difficulties for beginners:

with *"re"* series	with *"daal"* series	with *"jim"* series	with *"be"* series	letter
سر	سد	سج	سب	س
شر	شد	شج	شب	ش

Illustrations:

written form	components	word in transliteration
سِیانا	سِ + يِ + ن + ا + ا	*siyaanaa*
آسانی	آ + س + ا + ن + ي	*aasaanii*
بخشیش	ب + خ + ش + ي + ش	*bakhshiish*
شادی	ش + ا + د + ي	*shaadii*

پ + ا + س + ی   پاسی   *paasii*

Exercise 1

Read the words below:

ساتھی   دِشا   سونا   سوئے   آشا   خوشی   سَخاوت   سیتا   خاموش

سیاہا   شیلا   فِشان   قَسَم   گِلاس   ڈِسمِس   سپنا   سِتم   شب   شناسی

شانتی

Combine the following letters to create words indicated in parentheses:

(khuush) خ + و + ش	(siidhaa) س + ی + دھ + ا
(nashiid) نَ + ش + ی + د	(sacaaii) سَ + چ + ا + ء + ی
(mushaabaha) مُ + ش + ا + بَ + ہ + ہ	(baseraa) بَ + س + ے + ر + ا
(gustaakhii) گُ + س + ت + ا + خ + ی	(pesh waaii) پ + ے + ش + و + ا + ء + ی
(DhaaRas) ڈھ + ا + ڑَ + س	(tasaahul) تَ + س + ا + ہ + ل

Can you write these words in the Urdu script?

suuT	shaadii
suuTkes	mushaawarat
sitaar	gusaaii
kaashii	shafiiq
fasaad	daasharath

6.2 The *"swaad"* and *"to'e"* series

The *"swaad"* and *"to'e"* series consists of four letters which share the common feature of having

an oval shaped loop. For the *"swaad"* series, the line of script descends from the oval loop into a

curve (ص) while for the *"to'e"* series a vertical line is drawn to touch the loop at the left to

create a form that resembles the English "b" (ط). (We have seen a miniature version of this

letter being used as a superscript sign to indicate palatal and retroflex letters, i.e. ٹ ڈ ت). All

four letters are used to represent distinctive Arabic sounds occuring in certain words of Arabic or

Persian origin. However, most Urdu speakers, finding it difficult to pronounce these sounds in

the Arab manner, pronounce them according to the nearest Urdu equivalent. For instance,

"swaad" is pronounced as if it were *"siin,"* *"zwaad "* as if it were *"ze."* The letters of these

series are:

pronunciation	transliteration	name	letter
similar to English "s"*	s	*swaad*	ص
similar to English "z"**	z	*zwaad*	ض
similar to English "t"***	t	*to'e*	ط
similar to English "z"**	z	*zo'e*	ظ

*the letters used to indicate the "s" sound in Urdu are ص س ث

** the letters used to indicate the "z" sound in Urdu are ظ ض ز ذ

*** the more common letter for the dental "t" in Urdu is ت

The letters of the *"swaad"* and *"to'e"* are friendly. However, there is no difference in the initial,

medial and final forms of the *"to'e"* series:

end of word	middle of word	beginning of word	independent form	letter
ـص	ـصـ	صـ	ص	*swaad*
ـض	ـضـ	ضـ	ض	*zwaad*
ـط	ـطـ	طـ	ط	*to'e*
ـظ	ـظـ	ظـ	ظ	*zo'e*

The chart below shows the combination of these letters with long vowels:

with "*wao*"	with "*baRii ye*"	with "*choTii ye*"	with "*alif*"
صو	صے	صی	صا
ضو	ضے	ضی	ضا
طو	طے	طی	طا
ظو	ظے	ظی	ظا

Illustrations:

written form	components	word in transliteration
صورت	ص+و+ر+ت	*suurat*
ضرورت	ضَ+ر+و+ر+ت	*zaruurat*
طاق	ط+ا+ق	*taaq*
نظر	نَ+ظَ+ر	*nazar*

Exercise 2

Read the words below:

ظَهِير   طوفان   راضی   بِساط   خَط   صِفَر   خاص

إحاطہ   ضِیا   "خُدا حافِظ"   ضابِطہ   صَنَم   صَحِیح   فاضِل

Combine the following letters to form words indicated in parentheses:

(mazmuun) مَ + ض + م + و + ن   (tawaaif) طَ + ا + و + ءِ + ف

(hisaar) حِ + ص + ا + ر   (zamiir) ضَ + م + ي + ر

(taalib) طا + لِ + ب   (khitaab) خِ + ط + ا + ب

(ribaat) رِ + ب + ا + ط   (safaaii) صَ + ف + ا + ء + ي

(naziir) نَ + ظ + ي + ر   (zaahir) ظا + ہِ + ر

Can you write these words in Urdu?

sadaa (s="swaad")   *huzuurii (h="baRii he" z="zwaad")*

taarii (t= "to'e")   *qitaar (t="to'e")*

basiir (s="swaad")   *qaazii (z="zwaad")*

subah (s="swaad" h="baRii he")   *taair (t="to'e")*

zafar (z="zo'e")   *nizaam (z="zo'e")*

6.3 "*Nuun ghunna*" and nasalization

The term "*nuun ghunna*" means the "n that nasalizes." It refers to a letter of the Urdu script that

is used to indicate that a vowel should be nasalized, that is, it should be pronounced through the

50

nose. In its independent and final forms "nuun ghunna" resembles the letter "nuun" except that the dot in the center is omitted: ں. In English transliteration "nuun ghunna" is indicated by "n" with a dot above it. Thus ماں is transliterated "maaṅ"; زباں is transliterated "zabaaṅ." In its medial form, the "nuun ghunna" retains the dot in order to be legible. In this case, it is not distinguishable in writing from a regular "n" and only context indicates that nasalization exists. For example: پانچ is pronounced as "paaṅc," لنکا is pronounced as "laṅkaa." One way to distinguish a regular consonant "nuun" in the middle of a word from the "nuun ghunna" is that the former, being a consonant, can take a vowel while the latter cannot. "Nuun ghunna," when it precedes the letter "b" or "p," is often pronounced as "m": گنبد "gumbad" منبر "mimbar."

Exercise 3

Read the words below:

میں ہوں ہے ہیں ماں مہنگا گھنگھرو بنگال بانس

پتنگ لگن آشیاں گاؤں ذاتیں لڑکیاں

Combine the following letters to create the words indicated in parentheses:

(saunf) س+و+ں+ف   (saaṅp) س+ا+ں+پ

(umaṅg) اُ+م+ں+گ   (kaṅval) کَ+ں+وَ+ل

(jaauuṅ) ج+ا+ء+و+ں   (seṅtiis) س+ے+ں+ت+ي+س

(ciizeṅ) چ+ي+ز+ے+ں   (gunaahoṅ) گُ+ن+ا+ہ+و+ں

(kahaaṅ) کَ+ہ+ا+ں   (Dhaṅg) ڈَھ+ں+گ

Can you write these words in Urdu?

jaṅgal	*saaṅs*
aṅgrez	*vahaaṅ*
caaṅd	*saṅgh*
palaṅg	*paauuṅ*
duuṅ	*bhaaṅg*

Unit Seven

7.1 The letters "*ain*" and "*ghain*"

The letters "*ain*" and "*ghain*" occur exclusively in words of Arabic origin. In Arabic "*ain*" has a distinct sound. However, in Urdu, its pronunciation is variable and will be discussed below. The letter "*ghain*" is a voiced velar fricative articulated from the throat. It has a pronunciation similar to the French "r" in "Paris." In terms of their shapes, the independent forms of these letters begin with a shape resembling the number "2" in reverse which descends into a sharp curve similar to that of the "*jiim*" series. The letter "*ghain*" (غ) is distinguished from "*ain*" (ع) by a single superscript dot.

pronunciation	transliteration	name	letter
see note 7.2 below	'	*ain*	ع
similar to French "r"	<u>gh</u>	*ghain*	غ

As the chart below illustrates, both letters are friendly and change their shape according to their position in the word. The initial form of both letters consists of simply the reverse number "2" without the sharp curve. The medial form consists of a flat topped loop with sharp corners (rather than the more rounded loop of the letters "*fe*" and "*qaaf*"). The final form of "*ain*" and "*ghain*" is similar to that of the "*jiim*" series, the major difference being that "*ain*" and "*ghain*" have a characteristic flat topped loop with sharp corners.

end of word	middle of word	beginning of word	independent form	letter
ع	ـعـ	عـ	ع	*ain*
غ	ـغـ	غـ	غ	*ghain*

The chart shows the combination of *"ain"* and *"ghain"* with various vowels:

with " *wao*"	with "*baRii ye*"	with "*choTii ye*"	with "*alif*"
عو	ـع	عی	عا
غو	ـغ	غی	غا

Illustrations:

written form	components	word in transliteration
عَدالت	ع + د + ا + ل + ت	*'adaalat*
بَغَل	بَ + غَ + ل	*baghal*
بالِغ	ب + ا + لِ + غ	*baaligh*
شَعور	شَ + ع + و + ر	*sha'uur*

7.2 Note on pronunciation of *"ain"*

While the letter *"ain"* has a distinctive pronunciation in Arabic, in Urdu its pronunciation varies according to its context:

a) At the beginning of words it is usually equivalent to an *"alif,"* serving to carry a vowel.

For example, عِبادَت is pronounced as *"ibaadat"* and عَدالت is pronounced as *"adaalat."* The letter *"ain,"* when followed by *"alif,"* is pronounced as *"aa."* For example, عام is pronounced *"aam."*

b) After a vowel and before a consonant *"ain"* may modify the vowel in the following ways:

- short "a" vowel will be lengthened to long *"aa"* vowel e.g بَعد is pronounced *"baad."*

- short "i" vowel will become *"e"* e.g. اِعتِبار is pronounced *"etibaar."*

- short "u" vowel will become "o" e.g. شُعلـہ is pronounced "shola."

c) After a consonant at the end of a word, "ain" acts as an "alif" providing a long "aa" vowel sound. For example, جَمَع is pronounced "jamaa" and مَوقَع is pronounced "mawqaa."

d) In other situations, such as in between vowels, "ain" acts as a boundary marker (similar to "hamza") and is not pronounced, e.g. شَعور "shauur." After a consonant in the middle of a word, the "ain" is silent and has no impact on pronunciation, e.g مَشعَل "mashal."

Exercise 1

Read the words below:

عَورَت   بَغداد   غَلَط   عَظیم   شَمَع   جَماعت   شُروع   مَنَع   تَعریف

مُعجزہ   شِعر   جُمعرات   غَرَض   عَجائب   قِلعہ   شُعلے   تَعلیم   تَعطیل   صِفَت

طعنہ   غَیبَت   عیسائی   غائب

Can you write the following? (' indicates "ain")

ghaniimat za'iif (use ض for "z") 'aiinak ba'iid baghair baaghii 'aalam kaaghaz (use ز for "z") du'aa daregh mughal 'iraaq ghazal (use ز for "z")

7.3 Orthographic signs: the "jazm" or "sukuun"

The "jazm," which means literally "cutting short" or "keeping silence," is an orthographic sign placed above a consonant to indicate that there is no short vowel to be pronounced with it. There are a few alternative ways of indicating the "jazm," the most common being the superscript sign that resembles a small circle: ° . Since a vowel-less consonant is considered to be inert, the "jazm" is sometimes called "sukuun," meaning "still or stationary." The presence of a "jazm" over a consonant means that it has to be pronounced in conjunction with the consonant after it without any intervening vowel sound, forming a consonantal cluster. For example, دوسْت, the Urdu word for "friend," is pronounced "*dost"* with no vowel between the "s" and "t." Similarly, دَرْد , the Urdu word for "pain," is pronounced as "*dard."* As is the case with the other vowel diacritics, the "*jazm"* is only written in rare circumstances, as with foreign words or ambiguities. Normally, it is assumed that the reader understands, from prior knowledge and context, that a word includes a "*jazm.*"

<u>Note on the deletion of penultimate vowels while pronouncing certain words</u>

Several words in Urdu, ending in a consonant, contain the following arrangement of vowels (v) and consonants (C): vCvC. When, as a result of grammatical constructions, a long vowel is added after the word final consonant, the penultimate vowel (that is, the vowel between the two consonants) will not be pronounced, giving the impression that there is a *"jazm"* in the word. However, since this *"jazm"* is not intrinsic in the root of the word, it is never written. Examples:

1) The addition of an *"e"* vowel to the verb stem *"samajh,"* "to understand," results in the pronunciation *"samjhe,"* rather than *"samajhe."*

2) The addition of a nasalized *"oṅ"* vowel to the noun *"saRak,"* "street, road," results in the pronunciation *"saRkoṅ,"* rather than *"saRakoṅ."*

Exercise 2

Read the words below, all of which contain a *"jazm."*

دُرُسْت اصْلی اندر دُنْیا جانْور جُسْتجو اِسْٹیشن اِسْپیشل صِرْف

56

مَسْت ٹھَنڈا گُفْتگو مَطْلَب اِسْتِعداد اِقْتِصادی تَطْہیر اِسْتِعمال اِسْتِغْفار

Combine the following letters to form the words indicated in parentheses:

(sufl) ل + ف + شُ   (sust) س + س + تُ

(darakht) د + رَ + خ + ت   (sundar) س + ن + دَ + ر

(dharma) د + ر + مَ   (murgh) مُ + ر + غ

(Dhang) ڈ + ن + گ   ('umr) عُ + م + ر

(zikr) ذِ + ک + ر   (manzar) مَ + ن + ظ + ر

(prem) پ + ے + ر + م   (barf) بَ + ر + ف

(taksiir) تَ + ک + س + ی + ر   ('ishq) عِ + ش + ق

(jhanjhar) جھ + ن + جھ + ر   (zakhm) زَ + خ + م

(sabr) صَ + ب + ر   (jazm) جَ + ز + م

(qutb) قُ + ط + ب   (canDaal) چ + ن + ڈ + ا + ل

7.4 Orthographic signs: the *"tashdiid"*

The *"tashdiid"* is an orthographic sign resembling the English letter "w" that is placed above a

consonant: It indicates that the letter beneath it has to be repeated twice in pronunciation.

Thus, the Urdu word *"bacca,"* meaning "child," is written as بَچّہ rather than بَچہ The above

example demonstrates that the *"tashdiid"* over the letter "c" (چ) also has the effect of a *"jazm"* in

57

that the first "c" is pronounced without a vowel. The suppression of the vowel of the first consonant is, in fact, obligatory with the use of *"tashdiid."* A *"tashdiid"* over a consonant with *"do cashme he"* frequently means that the consonant is to be read in both its unaspirated and aspirated forms. For example, پتَّھر is read as *"patthar"* and اُچّھا is read as *"acchaa."* Finally, it should be noted that the *"tashdiid"* is never used in verbal infinitives in which two "n"s or *"nuun"*s come together, e.g. جاننا *"jaannaa"* = "to know."

Exercise 3

Read these words containing a *"tashdiid."* Remember that when reading doubled consonants there are no vowels between the first and second consonants.

غُصّہ   مُحمّد   ذِلّت   چِٹّھی   قِصّہ   کچّا   سِدّھی   پِلّا   کھَٹّا   قوّالی   ضِدّی

ظِلّہ   خَطّاط   کُتّا   بِلّی   حَجّام   فوّارہ

7.5 Orthographic signs: the *"tanwiin"*

The term *"tanwiin"* means "nunnation," that is, adding the letter "n" at the end of certain vowels. In Urdu it occurs in a few words borrowed from Arabic which are used adverbially. These words characteristically end with the *"an"* sound, that is, a short "a" vowel followed by the letter "n," an ending associated with the accusative case in Arabic. Rather than writing a short "a" vowel and a *"nuun,"* the *"tanwiin"* is used. This usually consists of an *"alif"* (even though the vowel is to be read as a short "a") with two small lines above it: اً Thus, فوراً is pronounced as *"fauran"* and حُکماً is pronounced *"hukman."* Note: with certain words, a *"hamza"* (ء) or the Arabic *"ta marbuta"* (ة) can be used in the *"tanwiin"* instead of *"alif,"* but these are extremely rare.

Exercise 4

Can you read the following words which all end in the "*tanwiin*"?

مَثَلًا یَقِینًا خُصوصًا تَقریبًا اِتّفاقًا عَمومًا قانونًا نَسلًا وَقتًا غالِبًا

قَطعًا لُطْفًا

7.6 Other orthographic signs

The following are common punctuation signs employed in the Urdu script:

period	۔
comma	،
semi-colon	؛
question mark	؟

7.7 Urdu numerals

The following chart shows the Urdu numerals from 0-12. Unlike the letters of the alphabet which are written right to left, the numerals are read left to right as in English. Thus ٢١ would be twenty-one while ١٢ would be twelve. Similarly, nineteen hundred and ninety-eight will be written as ١٩٩٨.

Urdu spelling	Name	Urdu numeral	numeral
صِفر	*sifar*	٠	0
ایک	*ek*	١	1
دو	*do*	٢	2
تین	*tiin*	٣	3
چار	*caar*	٤	4

59

پانچ	paanc	۵	5
چھ	che	۶	6
سات	saat	۷	7
آٹھ	aaTh	۸	8
نو	nau	۹	9
دس	das	۱۰	10
گیارہ	gyaaraa	۱۱	11
بارہ	baaraa	۱۲	12

Exercise 5

What are these numbers in English?

۵۷۸۲۳۹ ۳۳۲۱ ۷۲۸۰ ۳۷۲ ۱۷۶ ۸۲ ۹۰ ۴۳ ۵۴ ۷۸ ۷۵

Write these numbers in Urdu:

34 56 89 23 16 786 925 1073 4290 86217

Exercise 6

Can you read the names of these popular films?

۱۶۔ غُلام	۱۔ آوارہ
۱۷۔ گنگا جمنا	۲۔ ہم آپ کے ہیں کون؟
۱۸۔ ٹائٹینک	۳۔ دیوار
۱۹۔ تیرا جادو چل گیا	۴۔ مُقدّر کا سِکندر
۲۰۔ معصوم	۵۔ گلیڈ ی ایٹر
۲۱۔ ٹاپ گن	۶۔ کبھی کبھی
۲۲۔ گیس ہُوؤ اِس کمِنگ ٹو ڈِنر؟	۷۔ قیامت سے قیامت تک

60

۸۔ کہو نہ پیار ہے

۹۔ فِضا

۱۰۔ اِسٹار وارز

۱۱۔ گوڈ فادر

۱۲۔ اُمراؤ جان

۱۳۔ شری ۴۲۰

۱۴۔ شمع

۱۵۔ دِل والے دُلہنیا لے جائینگے

۲۳۔ راجہ ہندوستانی

۲۴۔ لو اِسٹوری

۲۵۔ پاکیزہ

۲۶۔ ریفیوجی

۲۷۔ سول مین

۲۸۔ مِشن کشمیر

۲۹۔ اِنجمن

۳۰۔ آئینہ

اردو رسم الخط مشقی کتاب

Urdu Script Workbook

Follow the direction of the arrows as you practice writing the letters

and words in this workbook.

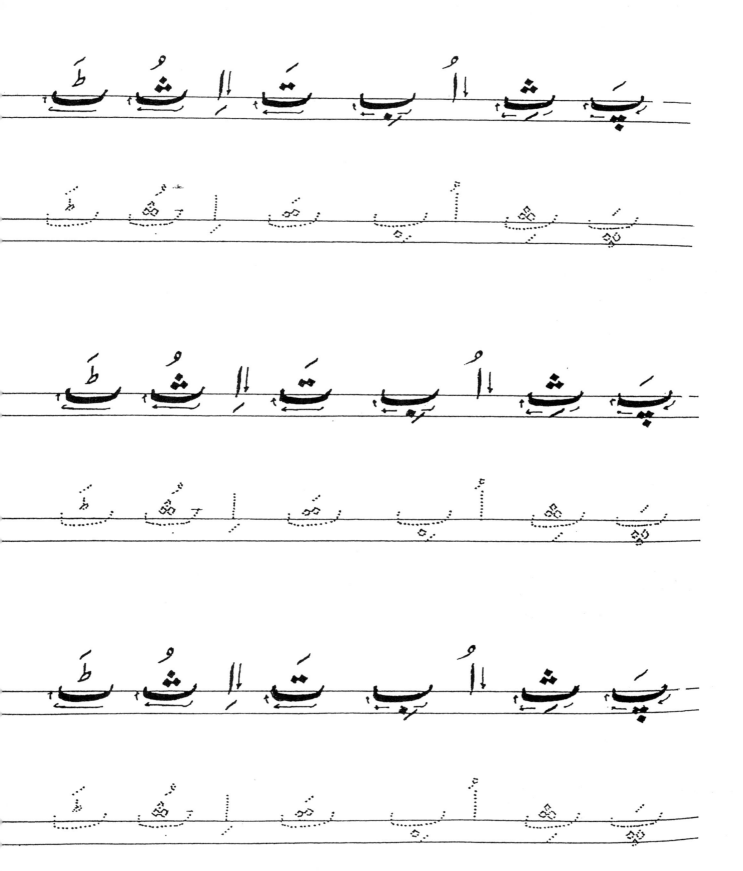

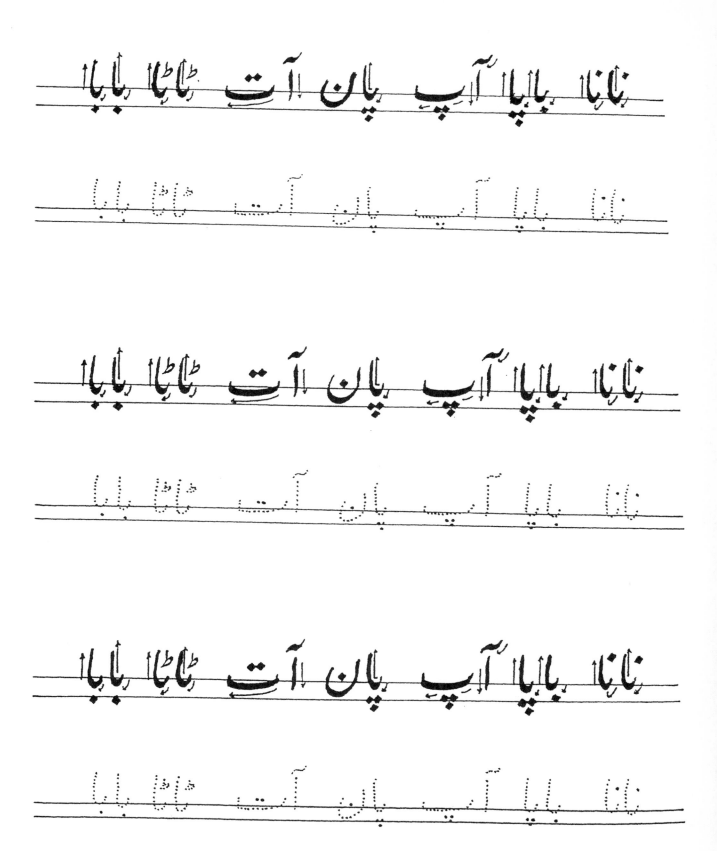

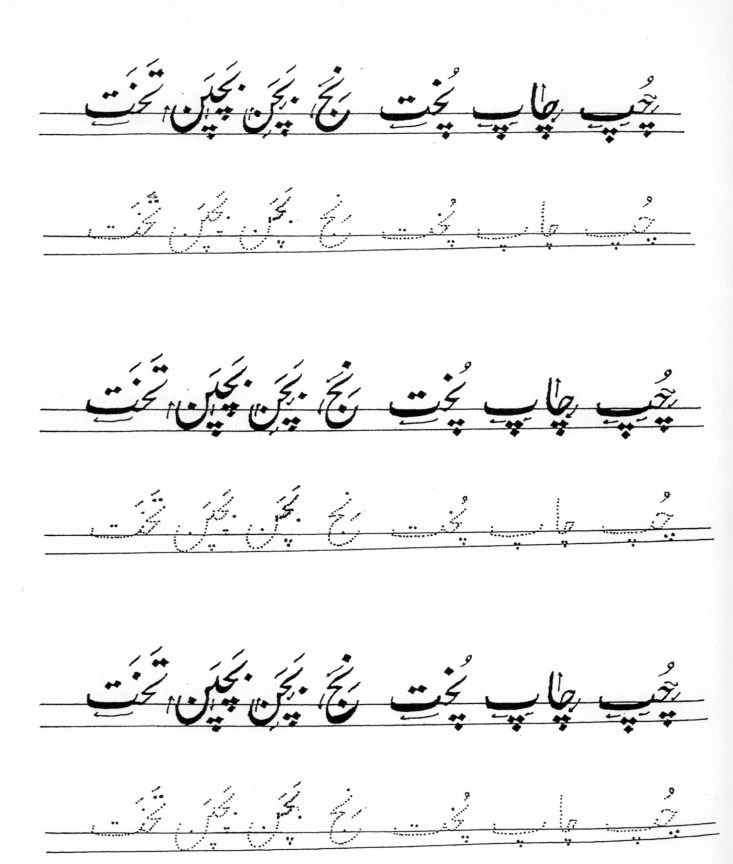

جی جی پاپی چاچی اَنّی چابی ناچی آپا

جی جی پاپی چاچی اَنّی چابی ناچی آپا

جی جی پاپی چاچی اَنّی چابی ناچی آپا

نا جا یا جا با جا حا جا خا جا پا جا تا جا

تا تا یا یا خا تا خا تا یا تا حا یا تا تا

نا جا یا جا حا جا با جا خا جا پا جا تا جا

تا تا یا یا خا تا خا تا یا تا حا یا تا تا

نا جا یا جا حا جا با جا خا جا پا جا تا جا

تا تا یا یا خا تا خا تا یا تا حا یا تا تا

وارج تاوان واجین واجبات واجی

واج تاوان واچن واجبات واجی

وارج تاوان واجین واجبات واجی

واج تاوان واچن واجبات واجی

وارج تاوان واجین واجبات واجی

واج تاوان واچن واجبات واجی

خاتُون پُوجا پاٹ پُوتا چوپٹ خُونی

خاتُون پُوجا پاٹ پُوتا چوپٹ خُونی

خاتُون پُوجا پاٹ پُوتا چوپٹ خُونی

خاتُون پُوجا پاٹ پُوتا چوپٹ خُونی

خاتُون پُوجا پاٹ پُوتا چوپٹ خُونی

خاتُون پُوجا پاٹ پُوتا چوپٹ خُونی

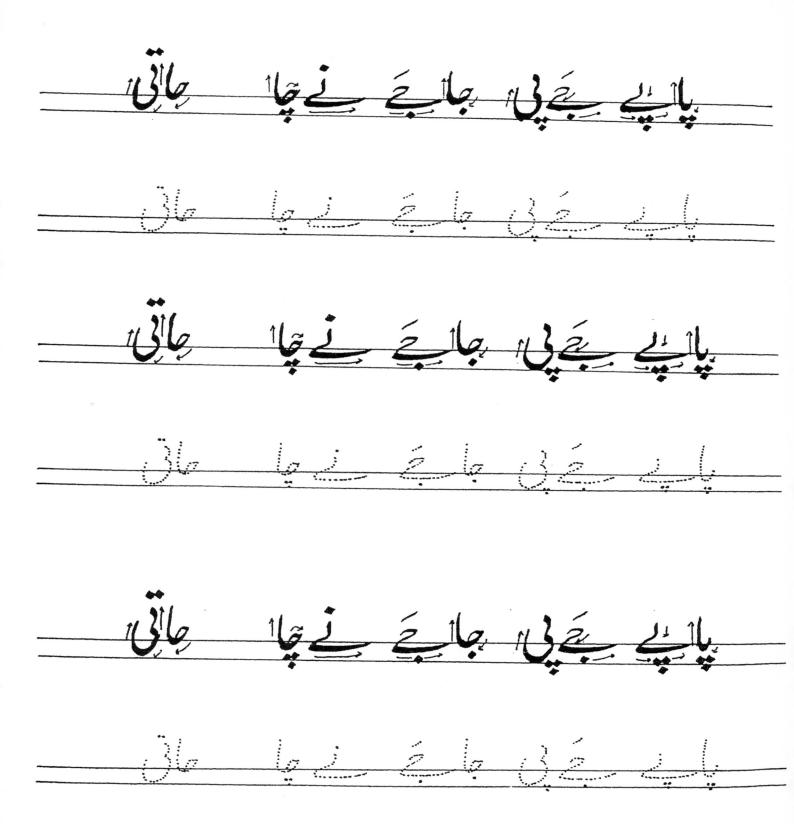

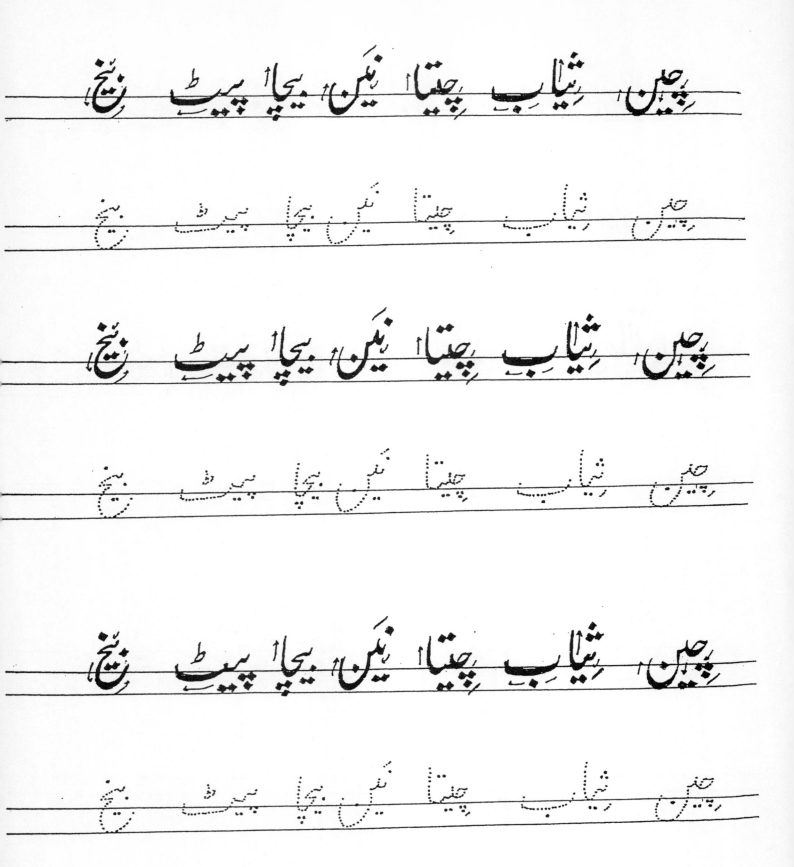

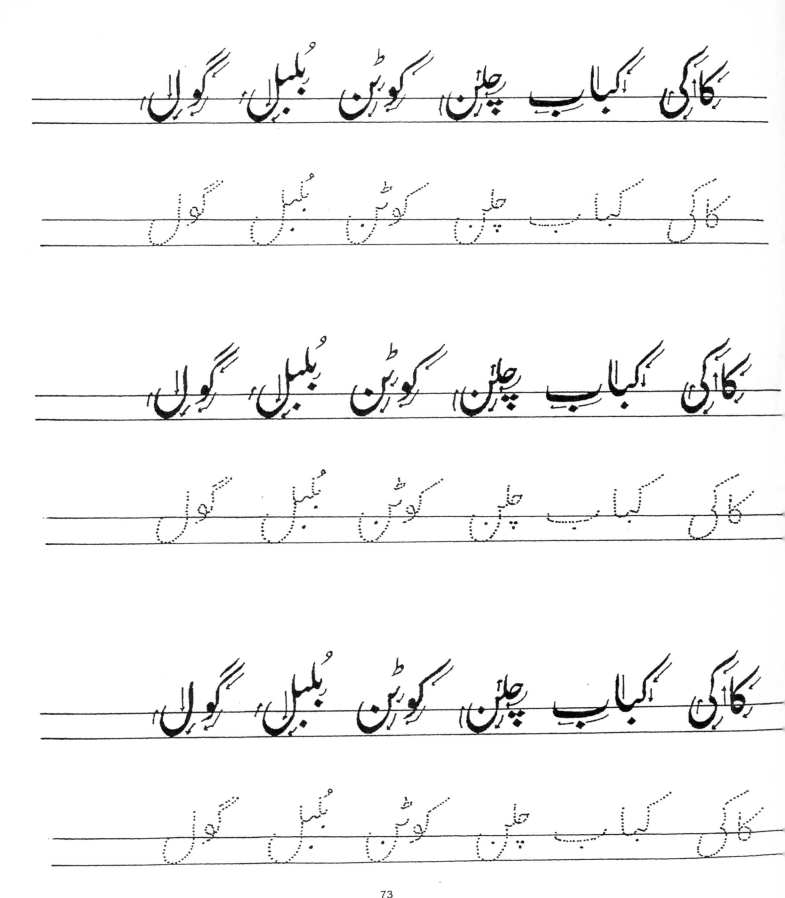

ذات رِ وادِی رُوڈاک کاذِب دے دے

ذات وادِی ڈاک کاذِب دے دے

ذات رِ وادِی رُوڈاک کاذِب دے دے

ذات وادِی ڈاک کاذِب دے دے

ذات رِ وادِی رُوڈاک کاذِب دے دے

ذات وادِی ڈاک کاذِب دے دے

اوج اَکیلا اَنیک آگے اَچج ایل

اوج اَکیلا اَنیک آگے اَچج ایل

اوج اَکیلا اَنیک آگے اَچج ایل

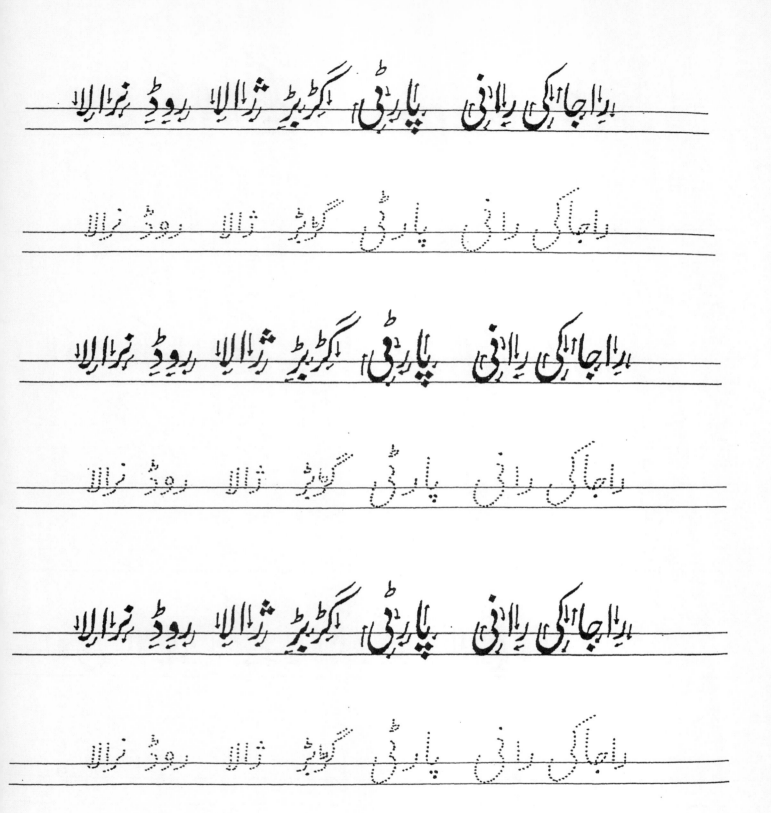

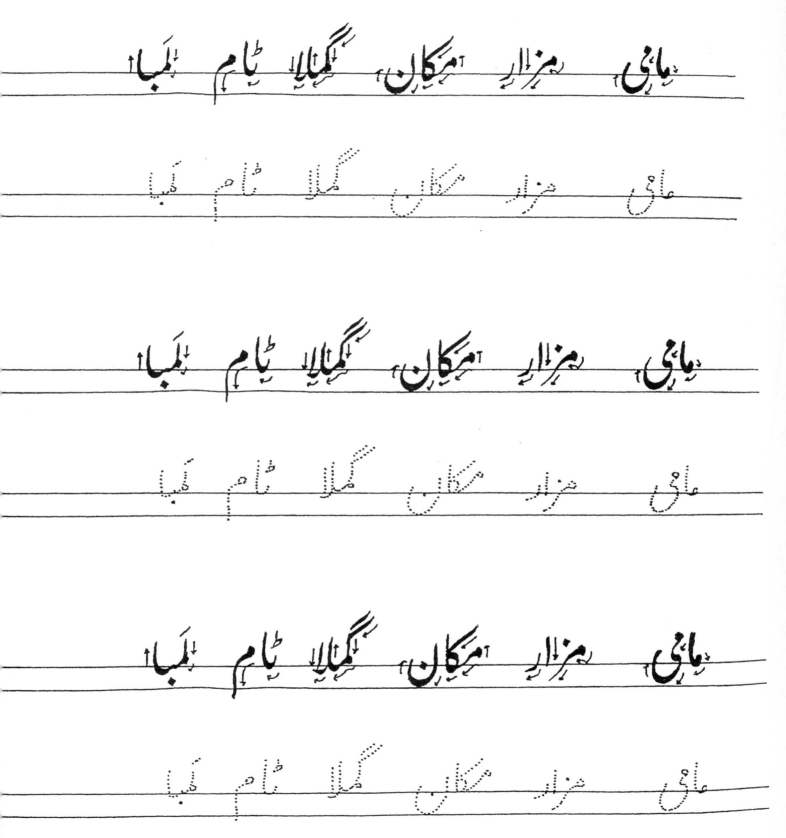

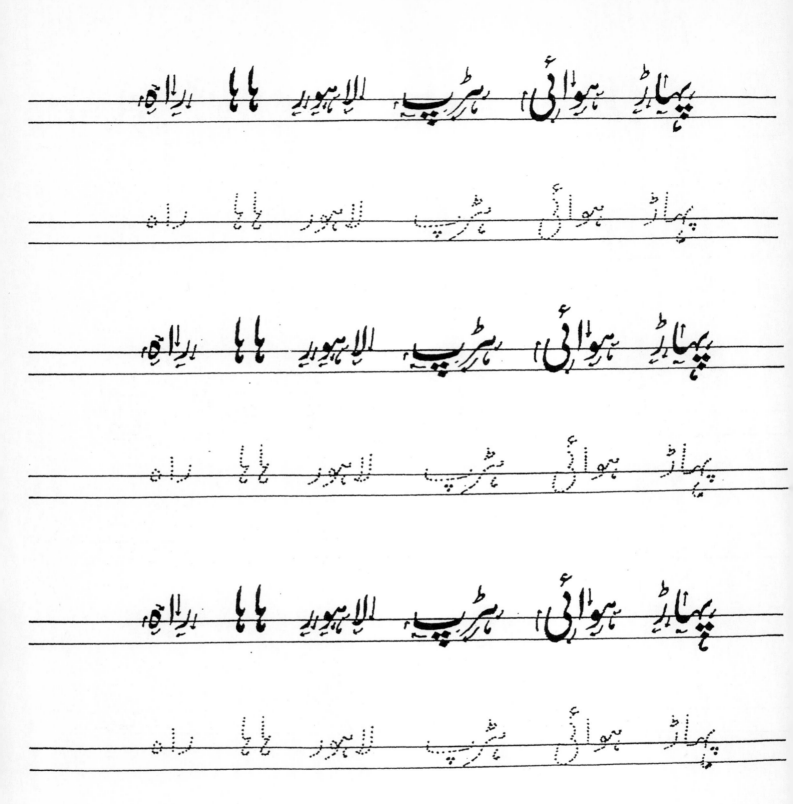

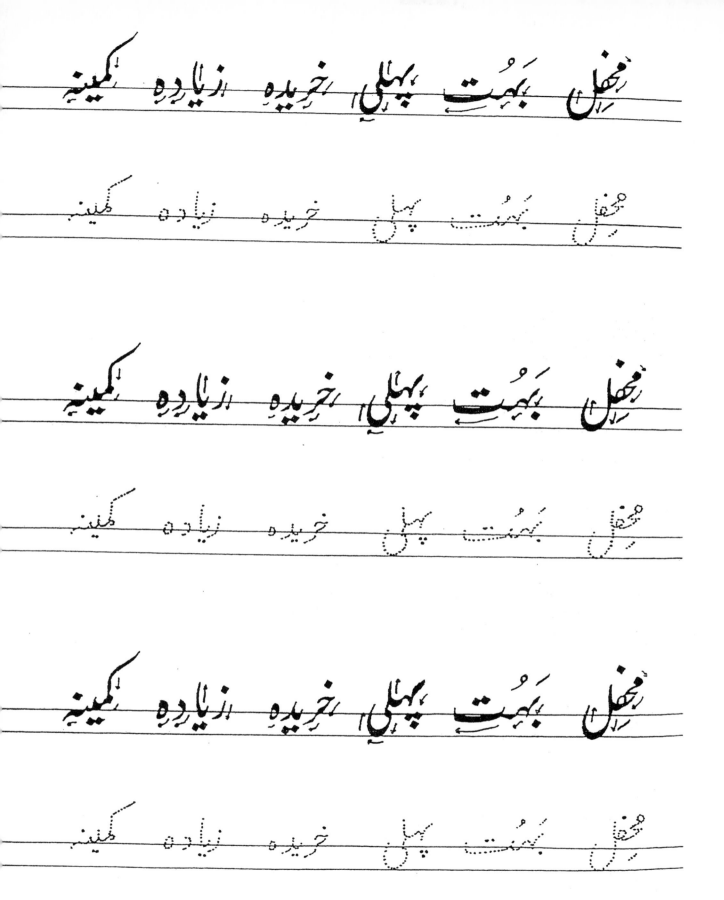

محفل بہت پہلی خریدہ زیادہ کمینہ

محفل بہت پہلی خریدہ زیادہ کمینہ

محفل بہت پہلی خریدہ زیادہ کمینہ

محفل بہت پہلی خریدہ زیادہ کمینہ

محفل بہت پہلی خریدہ زیادہ کمینہ

محفل بہت پہلی خریدہ زیادہ کمینہ

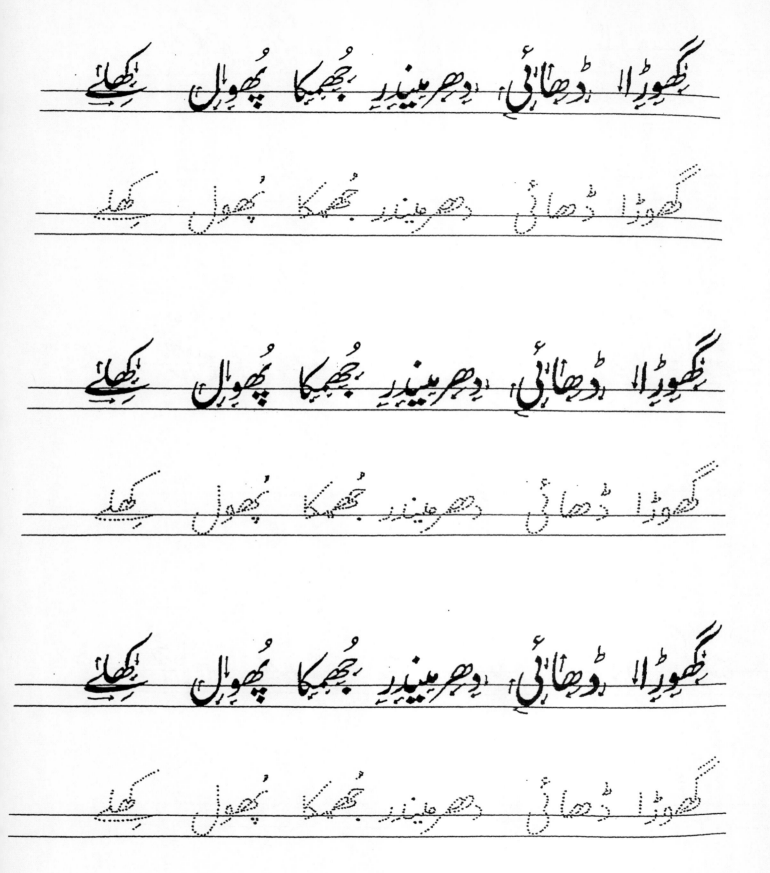

سخاوت رِیتا فِشاں قِسم ڈِسمس شانتی

سخاوت رِیتا فِشاں قِسم ڈِسمس شانتی

سخاوت رِیتا فِشاں قِسم ڈِسمس شانتی

سخاوت رِیتا فِشاں قِسم ڈِسمس شانتی

سخاوت رِیتا فِشاں قِسم ڈِسمس شانتی

سخاوت رِیتا فِشاں قِسم ڈِسمس شانتی

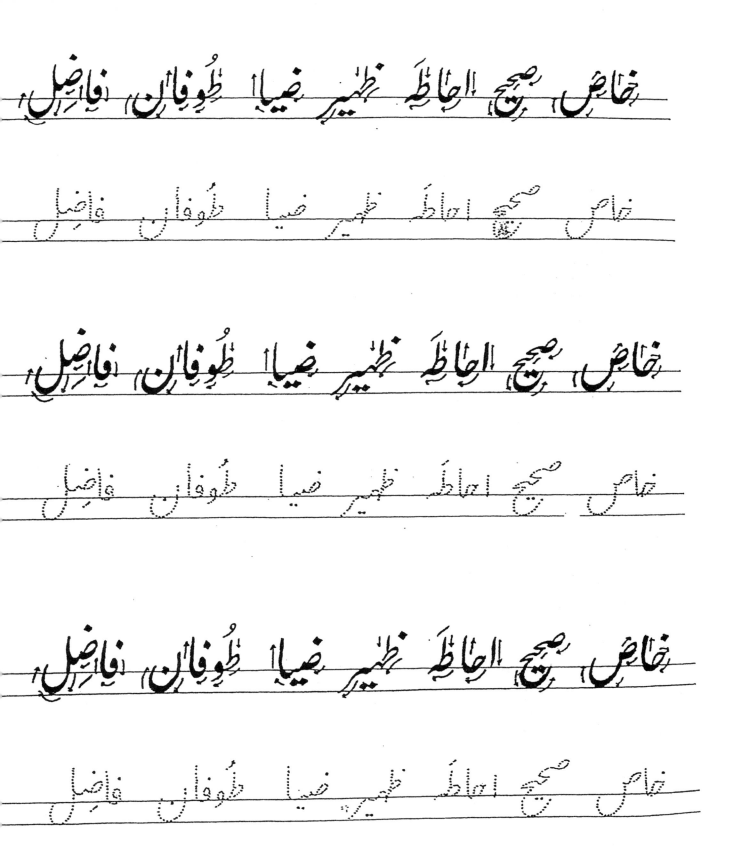

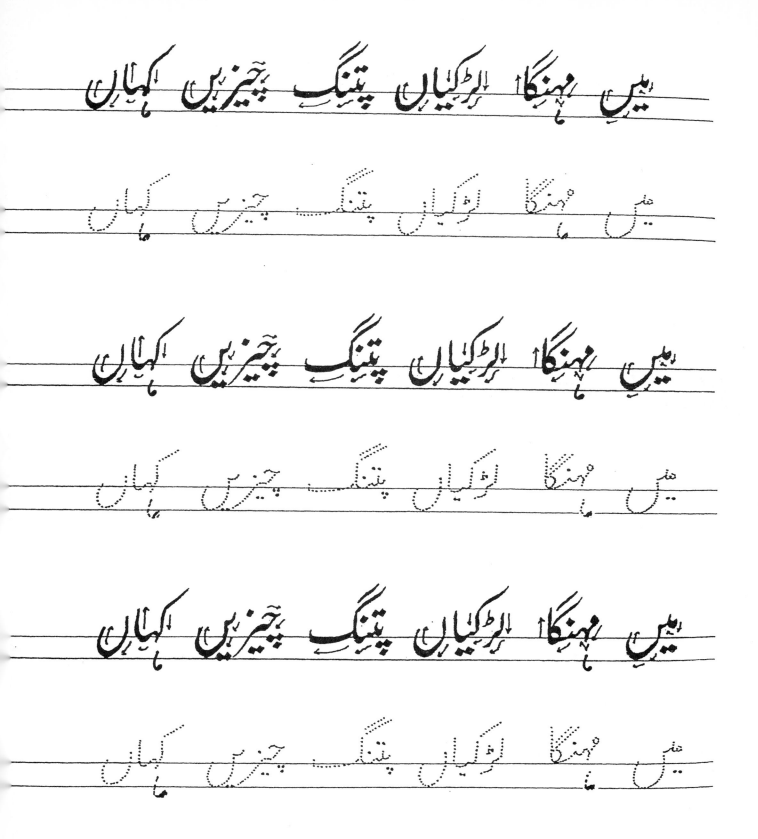

بغداد عجائب تعطيل غيبت عيسائى غلط

بغداد عجائب تعطيل غيبت عيساى غلط

بغداد عجائب تعطيل غيبت عيساى غلط

بغداد عجائب تعطيل غيبت عيساى غلط

بغداد عجائب تعطيل غيبت عيساى غلط

بغداد عجائب تعطيل غيبت عيساى غلط

استعداد اسپیشل اقتصادی استغفار دُنیا

استعداد اسپیشل اقتصادی استغفار دُنیا

استعداد اسپیشل اقتصادی استغفار دُنیا

استعداد اسپیشل اقتصادی استغفار دُنیا

استعداد اسپیشل اقتصادی استغفار دُنیا

استعداد اسپیشل اقتصادی استغفار دُنیا

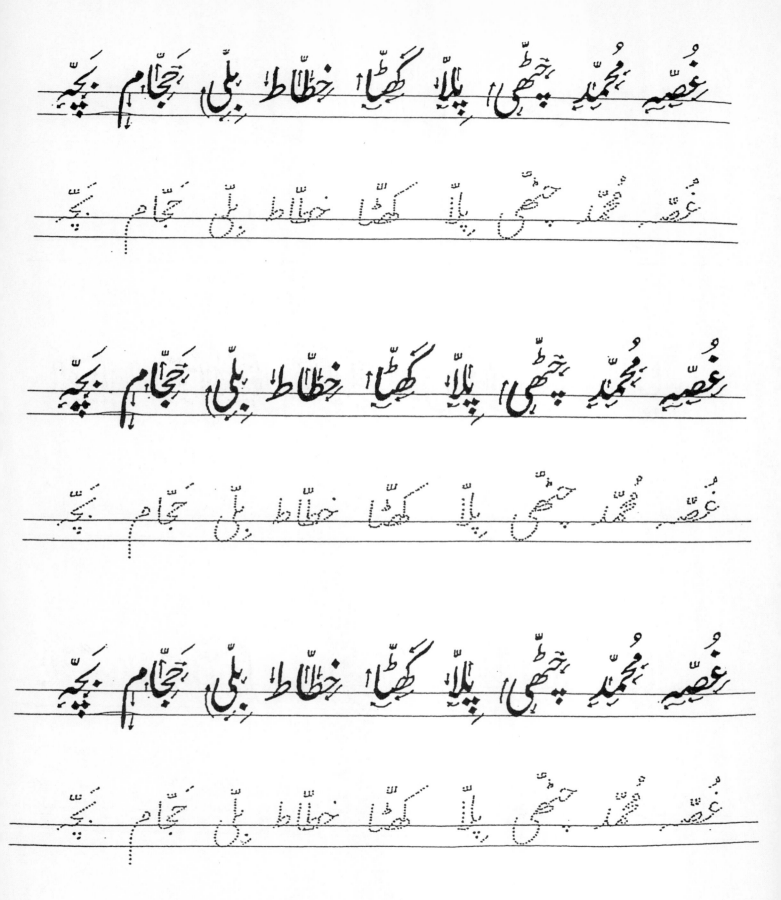

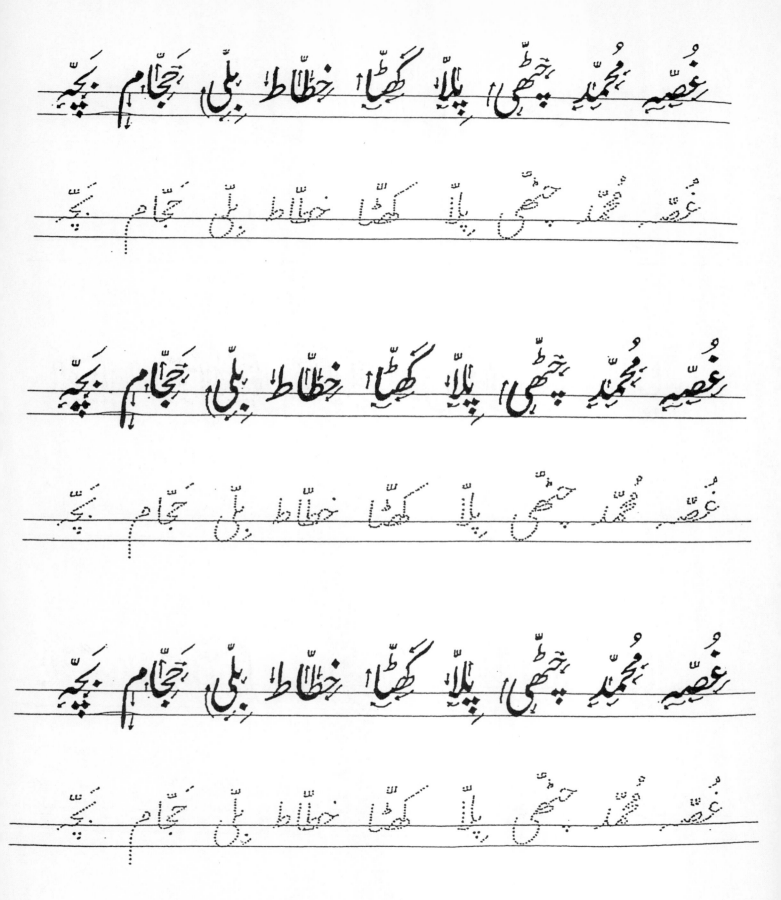

غُصّہ مُحمّد چھٹّی پلّا گھٹّا خطّاط بلّی حجّام بچّہ

غُصّہ مُحمّد چھٹّی پلّا گھٹّا خطّاط بلّی حجّام بچّہ

غُصّہ مُحمّد چھٹّی پلّا گھٹّا خطّاط بلّی حجّام بچّہ

غُصّہ مُحمّد چھٹّی پلّا گھٹّا خطّاط بلّی حجّام بچّہ

غُصّہ مُحمّد چھٹّی پلّا گھٹّا خطّاط بلّی حجّام بچّہ

غُصّہ مُحمّد چھٹّی پلّا گھٹّا خطّاط بلّی حجّام بچّہ

يَقِينًا وَقْتًا فَوْقًا غَالِبًا نَسْلًا قَطْعًا خُصُوصًا اِتِّفَاقًا

يَقِينًا وَقْتًا فَوْقًا غَالِبًا نَسْلًا قَطْعًا خُصُوصًا اِتِّفَاقًا

يَقِينًا وَقْتًا فَوْقًا غَالِبًا نَسْلًا قَطْعًا خُصُوصًا اِتِّفَاقًا

يَقِينًا وَقْتًا فَوْقًا غَالِبًا نَسْلًا قَطْعًا خُصُوصًا اِتِّفَاقًا

يَقِينًا وَقْتًا فَوْقًا غَالِبًا نَسْلًا قَطْعًا خُصُوصًا اِتِّفَاقًا

يَقِينًا وَقْتًا فَوْقًا غَالِبًا نَسْلًا قَطْعًا خُصُوصًا اِتِّفَاقًا